Houseplants

& indoor gardening

HOUSEPLANTS and INDOOR GARDENING

Series Concept: Robert J. Dolezal
Encyclopedia Concept: Barbara K. Dolezal
Managing Editor: Victoria Cebalo Irwin
Photography Editor: John M. Rickard
Designer: Jerry Simon
Layout Artist: Barbara K. Dolezal
Photoshop Artist: Gerald A. Bates
Horticulturist: Peggy Henry
Photo Stylist: Peggy Henry
Proofreader: Ken DellaPenta
Index: Alta Indexing Service, El Cerrito, CA

President/CEO: Michael Eleftheriou
Vice President/Publisher: Linda Ball
Vice President/Retail Sales & Marketing: Kevin Haas

Home Improvement/*Gardening*
Executive Editor: Bryan Trandem
Editorial Director: Jerri Farris
Creative Director: Tim Himsel
Managing Editor: Michelle Skudlarek

Created by: Dolezal & Associates,
in partnership with Creative Publishing international, Inc.,
in cooperation with Black & Decker.
BLACK&DECKER. is a trademark of the Black & Decker
Corporation and is used under license.

Library of Congress Cataloging-in-Publication Data

Bawden-Davis, Julie
  House plants & indoor gardening / Julie Bawden-Davis ; photographer, John M. Rickard.
    p. cm. -- (Black & Decker outdoor home)
  ISBN 1-58923-003-5
  1. House plants. 2. Indoor gardening. I. Title: House plants and indoor gardening. II.
II. Title. III. Series.
  SB419 .B23 2001
  635.9'65—dc21
                                        2001047614

ISBN 1–58923–003–5 (softcover)

PHOTOGRAPHY & ILLUSTRATION

PRINCIPAL PHOTOGRAPHY:
JOHN M. RICKARD: All photographs except where otherwise noted below.

OTHER PHOTOGRAPHY AND ILLUSTRATION:
KYLE CHESSER: pg. 55 (bot R).
ROBERT J. DOLEZAL: pgs. iv (top), 2 (top), 5 (bot), 86 (all).
IMAGEPOINT: pg. 6 (top L).
HORTICULTURAL PHOTOGRAPHY: pg. 90 (bot).
NETHERLAND FLOWER BULB INFORMATION CENTER: pg. 107 (top).

ILLUSTRATIONS: HILDEBRAND DESIGN

ACKNOWLEDGEMENTS

The editors acknowledge with grateful appreciation the contribution to this book of Brian Davis of Mt. Shasta Florist, Mt Shasta, CA; Merrile and Mary Herring, Sonoma, CA; La Petit Fleur, Pleasanton CA; and Betsy Niles, Sonoma, CA.

Houseplants
& indoor gardening

Author
Julie Bawden-Davis

Photographer
John M. Rickard

Series Concept
Robert J. Dolezal

*Decorating your home
with houseplants*

CREATIVE
PUBLISHING
international

MINNETONKA, MINNESOTA

www.creativepub.com

CONTENTS

INTRODUCTION

learned about the excitement of indoor growing at a young age. When I was 8 years old, I brought home a coleus, put it on a plant stand in a window, and checked on it every day. Within a few weeks it delighted me by putting out new growth. By the time I was 10, I'd filled just about every window in our home with houseplants, and I still wanted more.

For me, indoor growing is a daily adventure. I'm inspired every time I discover that an African violet is about to bloom, see an orchid spike, or witness a Venus's-flytrap closing. My houseplants have taught me that there is always hope. On many occasions I've thought I might lose a plant, only to be delighted to see it perk up again. Houseplants are not only resilient, they're a

*"A garden is
a grand teacher.
It teaches patience
and careful watchfulness;
it teaches industry
and thrift; above all,
it teaches entire trust."*

GERTRUDE JEKYLL

constant mystery. For me, every trip to the nursery and through a garden catalog is a journey worth taking.

While the pleasures of indoor growing are innumerable, one of the best aspects is that I forget about my cares when I'm tending my indoor garden. Time flies when I'm rearranging containers, measuring fertilizer, enjoying a fragrant bloom. Better still, I can work in my

indoor garden at any time of the year at any time of the day. It might be pouring outside or very hot, but I can always enjoy this perennial hobby. If it's late at night and I want to groom my houseplants (which happens quite often), I can do so. They are there every morning when I wake up and every night when I lay my head down to sleep, providing an endless show of quiet, lasting beauty.

The beauty of your home is enhanced and softened with living greenery and flowering houseplants

Beautify Your Home with Houseplants

The charm houseplants bring to home decor is one of the great advantages of growing them. With their wide variety of leaf shapes, sizes, colors, and textures, houseplants bring the natural world indoors and offer many different ornamental effects. They can be used to decorate just about any interior and serve a wide variety of design purposes—from adding a soft touch to a corner, to making a room look larger or smaller, to adding living color on a desktop, to simply making a room come alive and feel fresher. You can grow foliage plants, whose green leaves of multiple shapes, sizes, and tones are the center of attention, or branch out and cultivate blooming plants, some of which are fragrant.

Better still, indoor growing is a readily accessible hobby that can be enjoyed in the privacy of your home anywhere in the world. Although indoor climates vary somewhat, generally most interiors are very similar in temperature and humidity. Given similar lighting conditions, a snake plant can do just as well in Arizona as Alaska, and a pothos can vine its way up a wall in Montreal as vigorously as it would in Georgia.

Indoor growing also has something to offer everyone in the home—from children, who can learn much from the experience, to busier adults who find it to be a relaxing, fulfilling hobby. It is also an ideal pastime for those with physical limitations, as many of the activities can be done from a seated position at table height.

Houseplants pose very few challenges. Even if your home gets very little sunlight, you can choose from a variety of plants that can tolerate dim conditions; if you want to grow plants that require more light, you can obtain a lighting system that simulates sunlight, making it possible even to grow flowering plants.

In the pages that follow, you'll be inspired by the benefits of beautifying your interior with houseplants, and you'll receive all of the room-by-room guidance to create any type of indoor garden you desire, regardless of your locale.

This attractive room's appearance benefits greatly from the use of green houseplants. Try to imagine its appearance in their absence— chances are, its warmth and charm would be altered and the room would be less inviting. Make houseplants part of your home and take advantage of their many positive contributions.

ENTRANCES AND HALLWAYS

First impressions are important. Well-positioned houseplants have an immediate yet subtle way of putting people at ease, which is ideal when you and guests walk through the front door. A dramatic display of colorful flowering plants or a simple row of lush foliage creates a welcoming atmosphere and sets the tone for your entire home.

As you select plants to put near your front door, think high impact. Consider the available space and overall decor of your home and choose a plant or plants that give the visual message you wish to convey. Orchids are stately and give a formal feel, while African violets create more of a cottage-garden ambience. If you have the space, a tall grower such as *Dracaena fragrans* makes a striking first impression.

(Right) Housplants with soft profiles or weeping habits are good choices for narrow hallways. Here, a fern and a mixed planting of parlor palm provide relief from the hard tile floor.

(Below) Dress interior entries to a den, library, or formal dining room with a pair of plant stands that frame the passage.

You can also use houseplants to liven up hallways, which are often long and narrow. Small and vining plants are generally good choices because of space limitations. Put a basket with several small foliage plants on a side table, or highlight one showy foliage plant on a tall pedestal, or rotate in plants as they come into bloom, such as cyclamen, daffodils, and hyacinth. If your space is especially tight, train vining and climbing plants such as pothos or wandering Jew around a group of family photos and paintings, or hang a trailing plant from a wall-mounted container.

Indoor gardening in entrances and hallways poses few obstacles. The most challenging are drafts and temperature fluctuations caused by opening and closing the front door. These spaces also may be low on light, so keep that in mind when you select plants. *Cissus antarctica*, for instance, does best in cooler temperatures and will adapt to low light, as will cast-iron plant and English ivy.

Indoor plants offer intriguing decorating possibilities for staircases, transforming a climb to the second floor into a nature walk. The options are nearly endless.

A lipstick plant or goldfish plant hanging at the top of the stairs, for instance, makes for a striking accessory. Take advantage of narrow spaces by placing a large floor plant such as a dracaena or weeping fig at the stairs' landing, creating an attractive transition to other areas of the house. Add to the drama and architectural form of a staircase by growing a climbing or vining plant such as ivy up and down the stairwell's banister. You also can use plants of varied heights set on each stair to echo the geometry of the stairs. Or, on the wall below the staircase, attach a window box and plant a variety of pert, small plants such as polka-dot plant, radiator plant, or pickaback plant. A well-lit spot at the top of the stairs is a good place for a stunning illuminated focal point. Here you can display plants with bold, textured leaves, including begonia, caladium, coleus, or croton. This is also an excellent location for flowering houseplants such as anthuriums, orchids, African violets, or seasonal bloomers, such as flowering cacti and billbergia.

Your plant selections for stairways and landings will depend on your growing conditions. If the light is moderate or bright, you have more plants to choose from than if the light levels are low, but even in little light you can grow a surprising variety of plants. Various palms, ficus, and dracaena will tolerate low light and look especially good on landings. Among hanging plants, spider plant and some ferns will do well. And if you want the look of a certain plant that requires more light than is available, its easy to wire and install supplemental lighting.

When decorating staircases and landings, use care to make sure that the plants are kept out of the way of traffic to protect them from the damage caused when their foliage is brushed by passersby. Increase home safety by keeping the staircase clear and avoiding use of thorny or spiky cactus.

STAIRCASES AND LANDINGS

(Left) Use landings and corners to display tall foliage plants, greenery on a table or plant stand, and vines that trail into the passage below.

(Below) Mimic the form of an ascending staircase with a group of plants that step up in height along its banister.

KITCHENS

(Right) A bouquet of fresh herbs growing by the stove complements the chef's good taste and is a welcome addition to the flavor of savory meals.

(Below) Add a touch of color to your dining table's fruit center-piece by adding a potted African violet perched on a riser.

(Bottom) Many tall-ceiling rooms have ledges above the cabinets that are ideal for trailing plants, such as curly-leaved ivy.

The kitchen is the hub of family activity in most homes, and houseplants can make this room seem cozier. While just about any plant can grow in the kitchen, a selection of herbs does triple duty by cheering up the room and inspiring the cook as it provides fresh seasonings. Given adequate light most herbs do well indoors. Prostrate basil (during the summer months), bay, chamomile, mint, oregano, parsley, rosemary, sage, and thyme are all good choices. Because you need just a few herbs at a time, you can grow them in small pots or in a terra-cotta strawberry pot, which has separate planting holes all around the container. These containers make a decorative addition to the kitchen, and with their excellent drainage, they're suitable for herbs, which usually do best when kept on the dry side.

Large and airy new-style kitchens are ideal for a variety of plants. Many have built-in tiled windowsills where you can grow just about anything. If you have the space, a baker's rack brimming with colorful blooming and foliage plants also makes a cheerful statement. In smaller kitchens with less light, choose plants that require low light and let them drape down the refrigerator's side.

In general, humidity is higher in the kitchen than other areas of the home, so you can select plants that thrive in moist conditions. Be aware, however, that the humidity level normally drops during times when kitchen use is limited. Also keep in mind that cooking releases grease that may coat and smother plant leaves. Tough, glossy-leaved plants tend to hold up better than do those with softer, more delicate foliage. It helps to clean plant leaves on a regular basis by gently washing their foliage in water and allowing them to dry.

Remember practical requirements, too. Because the kitchen is primarily a working area, safety is paramount. Place all your plants away from the stove and oven, as well as other busy locations where they could become a hazard or suffer heat damage.

BATHS

The bathroom is one of the best places to grow many houseplants, especially those that flourish in the warmth and wet of a tropiclike setting. Homes often are dry, a condition that some plants tolerate poorly, while their bathrooms are usually humid. Thanks to this extra moisture, many houseplants do very well in bathrooms, provided that the windows are closed most of the time.

Houseplants also do wonders for a bathroom's decor. These rooms usually have a lot of hard lines and colors, with porcelain countertops and metal and brass fixtures. Plants soften the edges, making the room more inviting and relaxing. The combination of plants and water can be almost mesmerizing: taking a long, leisurely soak while gazing

at orchids on the edge of the tub or a Boston fern hanging from the ceiling can make you feel like you're enjoying a day at the spa.

Bathrooms have many suitable locations for plants. Besides tub-side or hanging from the ceiling or a wall, plants can sit on the back of the basin, next to the sink, on a plant stand, or on a windowsill.

Depending on your bathroom, lighting may pose a challenge. In fairly bright rooms, most plants will thrive. If the area is dim, consider changing your window treatments to let in more light, or look into supplemental lighting. You also can rotate plants to a sunnier location for a time and then bring them back to the bathroom.

Care of bathroom plants is about the same as for other houseplants, except for fertilizing. If your bathroom is small, you might want to curb plant growth. In that case, fertilize lightly on a monthly basis only during the warm months. Of course, for quicker growth—if you're trying to get a vine to drape from a window treatment, for example— you can fertilize at full strength. Just make sure to follow package directions carefully, water before and after you apply the fertilizer, and allow the plant to drain.

Several plants are excellent bathroom candidates: coleus, croton, Boston fern, maidenhair fern, creeping fig, flamingo flower, grape ivy, bamboo palm, trailing philodendron, pothos, prayer plant, spider plant, umbrella tree, and zebra plant. Several others are good visitors; give them a rest in an area with brighter light after they finish blooming.

(Left) Once rare and precious, the beauty of orchids is now an affordable luxury suited to the beauty of your bathroom. Moth orchids are long-blooming, sturdy plants with delicate floral sprays.

(Bottom) Your tub's surround is a welcome home to gardenia, a plant that needs little light but ample humidity. The aroma of its flowers will perfume the air as you bathe.

MASTER AND GUEST BEDROOMS

Though the master and guest bedrooms are used primarily for sleeping, they still have a place for a plant or two. Houseplants can bring a healthy, relaxed feeling to a bedroom with the added benefit of refreshing the air while you sleep.

Bedroom plants also offer myriad decorating possibilities. Well placed, a plant can make a bedroom seem cozier and more inviting, as does ivy growing across a canopy or headboard. Large floor plants such as dracaena, ficus, and palms growing in a corner near the bed lend an exotic, vacation-like feeling.

Foliage plants, with their vast array of color, shape, size, and texture, add another dimension to the bedroom. Leaves may be green, but they come in infinite shades and variegations, from light lime green to a green so dark that it almost looks black, as do the leaves of the rubber plant and *Peperomia caperata*. Leaf textures and shapes also vary considerably, from the glossy, heart-shaped leaves of anthurium to the soft, wispy foliage of asparagus fern.

Include houseplants in your overall design plan, blending them with your fabrics and wall coverings. Offset dark green curtains, for instance, with the mottled lime and medium green leaves of dieffenbachia or arrowhead vine. Use mosaic plant, with its white- or red-veined leaves, or the larger dragon tree, which has deep green foliage, to bring out the red in bedspreads and provide a contrast to flowing burgundy window treatments.

As long as you provide adequate light, the bedroom is an ideal place to mix flowering houseplants into the decor. Flowers come in most colors of the rainbow and in many different forms. Draw from the vast number of colors, textures, and shapes, and you'll find houseplants add to a bedroom's decor.

(Above) Epiphytes—plants that grow on bark or other plants and supply their nutritional needs from the air—are elegant, low-care accents, perfect companions to a bedroom.

(Right) Use plants in waterproof cachepots or plastic-lined baskets on dressers and end tables, taking care to protect their finishes.

(Below) It's always effective to match your houseplants to other decorative touches. Here, tuberous begonia's bright red coordinates with the fabric-art wall hanging.

Liven up children's rooms with plants. Let your imagination run wild, and have fun. When it comes to containers, think outside the box. Rather than planting in traditional containers, consider a pot made from children's play blocks, an old wooden train, or a small wagon. And opt for the unusual when you select plants. Kids love plants that are interactive or readily respond to stimuli. Venus's-flytrap is an excellent choice,

CHILDREN'S BEDROOMS

though some have been discarded prematurely when they entered their winter dormancy period. If there are no flies around, this plant just as readily will eat sow bugs, small spiders, or moths. Another plant that delights inquisitive minds is the sensitive plant; when you touch its ferny leaves, they fold and droop right before your eyes. Like the prayer plant, the sensitive plant closes its leaves at bedtime and reopens them in the morning—a treat for children of all ages. Plants that grow from kitchen scraps such as avocado, pineapple, and sweet potato also make good additions to a child's room. They are attractive plants that are fun for children to watch grow.

Terrariums make excellent projects for youngsters. Use an old aquarium instead of a bottle; the wide opening makes planting and care much easier. Think of building a terrarium as making a tiny garden. Add visual interest by mounding the soil to form little hills, and include various accessories that children treasure: rocks, polished stones, colored pebbles, marbles, small mirrors, and small ornaments, which make marvelous tiny gazing balls. You can even furnish the terrarium with doll furniture such as tables, chairs, and umbrellas.

Use caution when choosing plants for a child's room. Avoid including any plant that may pose a hazard when eaten or touched, and place plants with care since rambunctious play is likely. Good out-of-the-way locations for plants include unused corners, windowsills, the tops of dressers and bookcases, and hanging from a room's ceiling, secured to a sturdy hook.

(Above) The bright-colored blooms and texture of foliage make this flowering dahlia the right choice for decorating a young child's room.

(Left) Consider unusual plants such as African shield, a spathe flower relative, for a young boy's room. He'll be drawn by its curious, waxy, veined leaves.

(Below) Older girls may prefer surroundings that emphasize their feminine nature. Choose an unusual planting container and add a trailing plant such as the Swedish ivy grown in this whimsical tricycle basket.

DINING ROOMS

The dining room is often a location of relaxation and good conversation. You can make this room an even more pleasant place to linger by adding a few houseplants. How enjoyable to partake of delicious food with family and good friends in a room full of beautiful plants.

The table centerpiece often is the focal point of the room, so you'll probably want to place something dazzling here. In winter, highlight forced bulbs such as amaryllis, daffodil, hyacinth, paperwhite narcissus, and tulip. Rotate in plants as they come into bloom during the rest of the year—African violet, begonia, seasonal-flowering cactus, orchid. Or try plants with colorful foliage. Zebra plant is an eye-catching centerpiece with its vibrant striped foliage. Croton commands attention with its yellow, green, or purple pink leaves. An ivy topiary adds elegance, especially when it's trained onto a heart-shaped trellis. For a fun touch at a dinner party, include an edible centerpiece such as a pot of greens or seasoning herbs from which guests can pick and add to their plates.

Place settings are another opportunity to decorate the table with plants. Try small pots of individual crocus or adorn each place setting with 'Red Cap' cactus, polka-dot plant, or African violet.

Beyond the table, dining rooms offer many options for decorating with plants. Fill empty corners with large floor plants such as Japanese aralia, dracaena, ficus, palm, schefflera, and Swiss-cheese plant. Plants in corners of the room look especially stunning when they're dimly spotlit or hung with decorative strands of mini-lights.

Spruce up your furniture with greenery. Drape vining plants such as arrowhead vine, strawberry begonia, Swedish ivy, trailing philodendron, pothos, spider plant, and wandering Jew from a high china cabinet. Feature colorful plants on lower pieces such as hutches.

Match foliage and flowers with your furniture and fabrics. For instance, a purple velvet plant works well in rooms with lavender upholstery, while peace lilies will complement those with white and green tones.

(Top) A formal dining room will benefit from a graceful, long-flowering centerpiece, such as a phalaenopsis orchid.

(Middle) Informal kitchen nooks and dinettes, especially those in rooms with a country flair, look best with houseplants that bear bright blooms such as geranium.

(Above) Emphasize a room's theme by using decorative planters with a food or flower motif, such as this ceramic squash and cabbage companion.

(Right) Remember houseplants are for more than tabletops. A tall floor plant such as a parlor palm will unify the room.

Busy living rooms and sitting rooms also benefit greatly from the effects of houseplants. Plants may fulfill a variety of functions here: refreshing the air, adding vibrance, and softening the ambience. When choosing plants, start by considering your room's lighting. The light in sitting and living rooms varies widely, from bright areas with large windows to basement living areas with low light. Fortunately, you have plenty of plants from which to choose, whatever the lighting, since a surprisingly broad range of them thrive in low light; they include cast-iron plant, Chinese evergreen, dumb cane, elephant's-ear, fiddle-leaf fig, parlor palm, peperomia, pothos, prayer plant, rubber plant, sansevieria, and spider plant, among others.

SITTING AND LIVING ROOMS

(Left) Roses need bright sunlight to succeed as houseplants—at least 6 hours of direct sun each day is best. Place them near a window and closely monitor their health.

(Below) Use a waterproof plant stand to group plants that need a high-humidity environment. An island planter is a good choice to define the edge of an open room.

(Inset) Lightweight containers made of plastic resin give you the freedom to move your plants as you wish. Here, a tuberous begonia was reared in a greenhouse, then brought inside to display at the peak of its bloom.

Lighting is only one consideration. Your plant choices also will depend on the room's size. Big rooms give you a chance to add dramatic, large floor plants, such as the ponytail plant, which can grow to 15 feet (4.5 m) or more and looks especially eye-catching with its large, moplike head. Ti, *Cordyline terminalis*, is another good choice for an architectural, contrasting effect, as is the corn plant, or *Dracaena fragrans*, which lends a more casual, country look. Keep in mind that plants with long, drooping foliage make large rooms look smaller by drawing the eye upward, then back down to the floor. Place large plants in corners, or create a wall of plants behind a couch to create a junglelike setting.

To instead make a small room look larger, add tall floor plants and create a feeling of height and depth with bird-of-paradise, various palms, and rubber plant.

Smaller rooms can feel cozier with delicate, soft-leaved plants such as African violet, coleus, Boston fern, maidenhair fern, nerve plant, and radiator plant. Create intimate plant groupings on side tables with soft, touchable plants such as begonia, maidenhair fern, and purple velvet plant. On a coffee table, highlight specimen plants such as orchids and African violets or plants that make good conversation pieces such as Venus's-flytrap and sensitive plant.

Be creative in the living room. Hang plants or place them on tall furniture such as entertainment centers and bookcases, and let them trail down. Place a self-watering window box on a balcony. In a sunny window, create an indoor garden full of flowering plants.

Spice up rooms further by using plants to mirror other decor.

SUNROOMS AND SOLARIUMS

In the bright, airy atmosphere of a sunroom or solarium, you can grow just about any houseplant. Depending on how much sunlight the room gets and how it is heated, you also can cultivate a variety of plants generally grown outdoors in warmer climate zones—even citrus and banana. If you crave a junglelike setting with plants such as anthurium, bird-of-paradise, hoya, palms, and tillandsia, these are the perfect rooms. As a matter of fact, the more plants you pack into the room, the higher the humidity will be and the better these plants will fare. Or, you can create a forestlike setting with a variety of dracaena, ficus, Norfolk Island pine, and schefflera shading you as you sit on the sofa.

When planning a garden setting in a sunroom, mimic the design principles inherent in any natural landscape. The most effective look comes from varying heights, forms, and textures of plants. Include large floor plants, smaller plants on tables, and vines wherever you can. If possible, grow vines such as trailing philodendron and ivy from the ceiling; train them to move across walls and drape them from doorways and furniture.

Keep in mind that direct summer sun can dry and overheat plants in a sunroom, causing leaf scorch. Prevent this by installing blinds or light curtains. The type of heating system in your home also will affect your garden room during winter. If you have central air, you will need to create more humidity. More localized heat sources tend to be less drying and seldom lower the entire room's humidity level. Always check plants close to the heating unit carefully, however, since they may be the first to be affected by air that is too dry.

Also pay careful attention to your furniture choices for a sunroom. Because these rooms are very humid, avoid polished wood furniture. Better choices include plastic, rattan, cane, or rust-proof metal.

This sunroom combines several different elements—its rattan and wicker furniture, light and airy paint color, geometric tile flooring, and tropical foliage. It's easy to imagine settling down in one of the chairs to enjoy the room and its houseplants.

You've decided to try your hand at indoor gardening, so what steps should you take to successfully create the oasis of your dreams? A lush garden definitely is within your reach, but there are a few things to consider before you even bring any plants into your home.

Start by spending some time thinking about what sort of a garden you want and looking at what is available. You'll find fresh ideas in catalogs and periodicals, through electronic information sources, and in the nursery or garden center, as well as in the homes of friends and acquaintances. While your houseplants will be spared exposure to wind, rain, or snow, they will be affected by your indoor climate. This chapter explains how your environment affects the type of plants you choose and the way in which you use plants in your home. You'll also learn how to select containers, considering drainage, materials, size, and scale. Understanding how your site and houseplants interact will set the stage for success.

Of course, to have a robust, eye-catching garden, it's important that you start with healthy houseplants, consider each plant's habit and form, and acclimatize them to their new surroundings. In the following pages, you'll learn what tools and materials are needed for your indoor garden, as well as where to go for your plants and supplies, and you'll find instructions for selecting pest- and disease-free plants that will thrive in your home.

Once you've covered the basics and completed the planning process, you'll look at many important aspects of successfully growing lush houseplants, including key information about common house-plant care needs such as light, watering, fertilizing, air circulation, humidity, proper location, suitable containers, and plant supports and stands. You'll also see how you can incorporate houseplants into your overall decorating scheme.

Finally, this chapter ends with a flowchart, a list of questions designed to help you streamline the decision-making process as you begin your indoor garden.

> **Learn the basics of indoor gardening and decide how houseplants can satisfy your needs as you create a living home decor**

Checklist for Gardening Indoors

Every room of your home contains mixed growing conditions, each suited to different houseplants' needs. In general, flowering plants prefer bright light, while green foliage plants can adapt to the filtered sun or partial shade found in the corners of a room or away from its windows.

UNDERSTANDING INDOOR CLIMATES

In order to create a garden full of healthy plants, it's important to understand your environment. True, indoor climates are generally more constant than the outdoors, but atmospheric and light issues still play a role. Every house is different, and the environment can vary from room to room and season to season. Consider several factors throughout your home that affect your plants, including relative humidity, air circulation, temperature, and lighting.

Most homes tend to be dry, but many popular houseplants do best with a little extra humidity. Even when other environmental factors are ideal, plants that are challenged by low atmospheric humidity will exhibit sluggish growth, yellowing leaves or brown tips, leaf curling, and flower drop. You should learn the particular humidity needs of your plants, and become aware of the available humidity in your home. This is affected by several factors, including your location. Indoor air humidity in South Carolina, for instance, is going to be higher than that in a home located in Arizona or Quebec. The season also affects moisture levels. While Minnesota summers may be fairly moist, winters in heated rooms tend to be very dry. Air-conditioning tends to reduce humidity, too. Air moisture levels may vary greatly from one area of the house to another. Rooms with water—bathrooms, kitchens, basements, and laundry rooms—are usually the most humid. And the more plants you have grouped into a room—such as a sunroom—the more humid its air will become.

(Right) Air circulation will affect the health of your houseplants. Because the air from heat and air-conditioning registers often is drying, move your plants away from floor and ceiling vents.

(Below) Make misting a regular part of your care routine for those plants that prefer high-humidity environments. Misting removes oily deposits and helps the plant eliminate wastes in addition to giving them needed moisture.

In general, houseplants require at least 40 percent humidity. You can test the moisture level of the air in your home with a hygrometer, an easy-to-use instrument that can be found at some nurseries and hardware stores and through direct merchants. Get a good overall representative reading by testing the air in the room as a whole, and then check the air close to a plant. While the humidity nearest the plant is your most crucial number, remember that overall humidity in the room will still affect the plant. When higher humidity is needed, you can raise it by any of a variety of techniques: misting, grouping plants, mulching, creating a humidity tray—a tray filled with pebbles and water— or even running a humidifier near your plants or placing them adjacent to an indoor fountain [see Humidity and Air Circulation, pg. 34].

Air circulation is another consideration because plants need fresh air to prevent diseases and insect infestations. The amount of air movement required is minimal, though; plants' leaves dry out in overly drafty areas.

In many homes, there's enough circulation created by you and your family's movement or the opening and closing of doors. If your plants seem to be showing symptoms of stagnant air, which may include developing fungal diseases, try moving them to a location with better air circulation.

Temperature in the home also affects the health of houseplants. Fortunately, if you feel comfortable in your home, most plants will do fine. The average house-plant requires temperatures of 65–75°F (18–24°C). Certain plants, however, need periods with a change in temperature. Bulbs, flowering cacti, various orchids, strawberry begonia, and cyclamen, for instance, require winter temperatures of 50–65°F (10–18°C). For these, seek out cooler spots in your home, which include near windows that receive little direct sunlight—especially between curtains and the windows —unheated rooms, basements, or locations close to the floor. Avoid hot spots—near stoves, ovens, radiators, heating ducts, television sets, and high perches. The opposite goes for plants that require warm conditions such as wax begonia, lipstick plant, and ponytail palm. You can gauge the highs and lows in your home with a thermometer. Take readings in a room at different points in time to obtain valuable care information, informally noting the data for future reference.

Lighting is important to plants as well, and like temperature and humidity, it varies throughout your home. The closer you can match a plant with the light it needs, the better it will grow [see Light Sources and Quality, pg. 32]. Generally, fruiting and blooming houseplants need more light than those with solid green foliage, as do plants with variegated foliage. A plant's location in the home will determine the light it receives. An unobstructed window that gets direct sunlight most of the day, for instance, will be much brighter than one on the other side of the house. Windows to the East can be counted on for good morning light. Even bright rooms usually have dimmer areas, often located near the sides of the windows and in its opposite corners.

Keep in mind that light varies with the seasons, changing with the position of the sun. Consider the different light levels around your home and then match the light in each location with plant needs.

When sufficient natural light is unavailable for the type of plants you want to grow, you can use supplemental lighting, which can increase greatly the number of plants you grow. Although regular incandescent bulbs seem a logical solution, they actually have drawbacks as supplemental lighting because they emit only some parts of the lighting spectrum and plants need a full spectrum of light. Make your choice from several types of lighting, including fluorescent lighting, so-called grow lights, and High Intensity Discharge Light Systems (HID). When using artificial lighting, attempt to simulate daylight by giving plants regular periods of light and dark. Most plants do best with 12–16 hours of light per day. If necessary, use a timer to control the lights so that they provide your plants with the proper number of hours of light. Also educate yourself on how close you should position the lamps to each plant. This will vary according to the plant and the type of lighting system and can range from 6–48 inches (15–120 cm). After placing your lights, monitor your plants carefully for the first several weeks and adjust them as necessary.

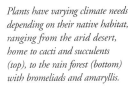

Plants have varying climate needs depending on their native habitat, ranging from the arid desert, home to cacti and succulents (top), to the rain forest (bottom) with bromeliads and amaryllis.

ACHIEVING A PURPOSE

Knowing what it is you want to accomplish with your indoor garden is your first step toward achieving a pleasing interior. Ask yourself some questions: Do you want plants throughout the house? Will you be concentrating on certain rooms? Do you dream of a tropical, junglelike interior, or is a sleek, more modern look your ideal? Deciding on the look you want to achieve before you collect plants saves both time and resources, as well as wear and tear on your budget.

Make a list of the goals you have set for your indoor garden. Perhaps you would like to create an eye-catching focal point indoors that can be seen through windows from outside. This can be done with a Boston fern hanging in a front room, which visitors can appreciate as they approach your home's entry. Or maybe you'd prefer to screen the view outside but want to avoid curtains. Set a vining plant on a windowsill or provide a trellis, and you will have created a living window screen.

You also can use plants to change the size perception of a room. Tall plants in a small room, for instance, make the ceiling seem higher than it is. Conversely, a short, wide plant that flows downward can make a large room look smaller by drawing your eye to the floor.

Perhaps you have dreamed of an indoor garden that gives you blooms, fragrance, and maybe even fruit. Although they need more light and have specific temperature requirements, flowering and fruiting plants such as citrus and banana are among those that can thrive indoors.

(Above) Plants are extensions of one's own sense of style. A formal pot of spathe flowers perched on an ornate stand conveys taste and elegance. Decide your purpose and follow a theme as sure ways to achieve success when you decorate your home with houseplants.

(Right) Your purpose may be as simple as adding a cheerful touch to a guest bedroom.

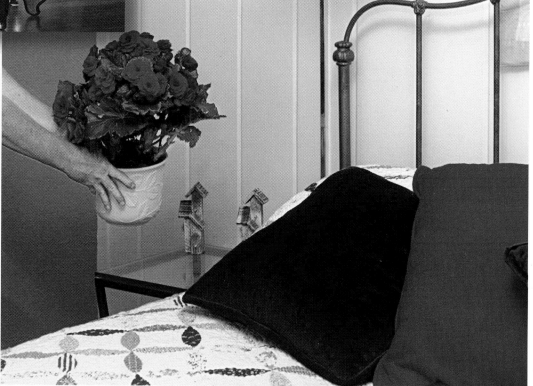

SIZE AND SCALE

Your indoor garden can be compact—a kitchen window garden, say, that takes minutes a day to maintain—or housewide with plants in every room, requiring greater commitment and care. Possibilities abound when it comes to houseplants. You can grow large-scale floor plants, hanging and vining plants, or small pots for windowsills and furniture. When narrowing down your choices, consider two main factors: how much room you have for plants and how much time you have to care for them.

As you select plants for indoor growth and display, pay careful attention to the plants' eventual sizes. While some will stay small indefinitely, others may eventually touch your ceiling. Many vining plants also can reach impressive lengths. If you plan to keep a plant in your home for an extended period of time, note these habits as you choose.

Another consideration is the amount of leisure time you have available for plant care. Indoor growing is a hobby that requires some investment of your time, energy, and resources. Gardeners who are new to the houseplant world should start small with a few plants in one room. As you master the care of these plants and become accustomed to the requirements of indoor growing, you can branch out into new areas with new plants.

Also examine your lifestyle. Do you take long vacations or frequent business trips that may interrupt plant care? If so, do you have backup care available? Should you set up a watering system that will tend the plants in your absence? Look closely at your world to see how good a fit your time and activities make with houseplants.

Your indoor garden may be as small as a terrarium (above) or as grand as a sunroom filled with exotic tropical foliage (below).

CONTAINER CHOICES

One of the most important decisions you'll make as an indoor gardener is in what containers you'll grow your houseplants. Choices vary widely, from decorated ceramic pots to those made of terra cotta, plastic, brass, and wicker. The style and type of pot you choose often depends on your decor. Besides aesthetics, however, you'll need to keep a few functional points in mind.

Drainage is a significant consideration; good drainage and ample drain holes are imperative. If your pot lacks drainage holes, drill some yourself or use the pot as a cachepot—a decorative container designed to hold an inner pot. Ceramic and metal containers make attractive cachepots, as do wicker baskets. Remember to line baskets with plastic to avoid fungal disease and moisture damage to other furnishings. To allow for good air circulation, the cachepot should be at least 1 inch (25 mm) bigger in diameter than the interior pot. Elevate inner pots on inverted saucers, if necessary, and always remember to remove any water that drains into the cachepot.

Size also is important when it comes to planting containers. Your pot should hold enough soil to accommodate a healthy root system and still leave 1 inch (25 mm) of room above the soil—known as headspace—for watering. Some plants such as succulents and cacti have shallow roots, while large plants such as dracaenas and ficus need more root room. The pot size should match each particular plant visually as well.

A good design principle is that the pot should be one-third the height of the plant/container combination. Avoid potting in containers that are too large, because soil surrounding the roots can hold excess moisture, which could lead to fungal disease.

Size and drainage are but two considerations when selecting containers. You also need to choose the materials from which they're made. While various containers are available, clay and plastic seem to be the most popular.

Clay pots are easy to find and come in many shapes, sizes, and colors, including brown, gold, green, red, purple, and terra cotta. Styles vary, from plain containers, to Greek pots, to vases with designs that include grapes, fish, sun rays, and iguanas. Some planters are even shaped like animals such as swans, frogs, fish, turtles, and hippos.

A close cousin to clay is ceramic. Whereas clay pottery is usually fired in a kiln and then painted, ceramic pottery gets its shiny coating from being fired, painted with glaze, and fired again. Like clay pots, ceramic containers come in a wide range of colors, styles, and designs.

Clay and ceramic pots are porous and breathe; they absorb moisture and permit air circulation. Because the walls allow evaporation, plants in clay containers need more frequent watering than those in plastic pots. For plants that require excellent drainage and dry conditions, clay is the best type of pot to use. Heavy clay containers also do an excellent job of anchoring top-heavy plants.

When using clay and ceramic pottery be sure to protect your furniture from water stains. Evaporation from such pots can leave mineral deposits on their surface, which appear as white rings that can mar furniture. These rings are often an indication that it is time to leach your plant containers to remove mineral and

salt buildup [see Deep Watering Houseplants, pg. 69].

Many gardeners choose plastic containers as an alternative, because they are free of water stains. Plastic containers come in dozens of colors, sizes, shapes, and styles. They are easy to clean, sturdy, lightweight, and economical. Many resemble terra cotta and can be used in a wide variety of decors.

Plastic pots often are preferable because they retain moisture more easily than terra-cotta and ceramic pots, which means their plants need less frequent waterings. In fact, since soil stays damp longer in plastic, these containers are best used with plants that require high moisture levels. Because they are lightweight, they are carefree, suited for hanging, and are visually appropriate for airy plants.

Some plastic pots have the added advantage of a built-in watering system with a reservoir below that provides water to the plant as it needs it. Depending on the container and type of plant, you can space waterings as long as every 2 weeks. Keep in mind, however, that self-watering pots are appropriate only for those plants that require continuously moist soil.

After considering these basics, your container choices will depend on your decor. When selecting a pot, look for those that not only complement your room, but also are suitable for the plants. For a delicate fern, pass by a big, heavy clay pot, and try instead a sleeker green ceramic container. A basket filled with plants may appear too casual for a formal dining room, but make a delightful addition to a den or family room.

To prevent water runoff on furniture and floors, use a saucer or cachepot, or water your plants outdoors or in a sink and let them drain thoroughly before putting them back in their usual location. It's also a good idea to create a waterproof buffer between the pot or saucer and the table or floor with a cork or rubber mat, or elevate the pot with planter feet, blocks of wood, or a wooden plant holder to help protect your floor covering from water stains and permit air to circulate beneath the container.

(Opposite pg.) Plant containers range from glazed and fired ceramic (top), to wood (middle) and plastic (bottom).

(Left top) Hardware stores, garden centers, and nurseries offer a wide selection of both functional and decorative pots for houseplants.

(Left bottom) Concrete and resin containers have the advantage of being both lightweight and waterproof, making them practical for indoor use. Here, concrete mimics a ceramic planter.

(Below) Large plants in heavy containers can be a challenge to move. Putting them on a sturdy, roller-equipped plant tray is an option worth considering.

PLANT HABIT AND FORM

(Right) Some plants naturally grow with trailing stems such as this oakleaf ivy. Their pendulous habit makes them ideal for use as hanging plants and on ledges.

(Below) Split-leaf philodendron begins growing as a bushy shrub. In time, it will extend its long tendrils high overhead.

A well-designed indoor garden has a wide variety of plants with various growth habits and shapes. To create a pleasing interior, combine small potted plants on tables and windowsills, cascading or climbing plants for vertical interest, and tall, striking floor plants for filling in corners and establishing transitions between areas of your home. When choosing your plants, consider all the options provided by plant growth habits and shapes.

Airy, feathery houseplants soften a setting, giving a room a more natural feeling. Good plants for this purpose include a wide variety of ferns, such as Boston and asparagus. Rounded, bushy, shrublike plants generally do a good job of adding interest to a room and filling in empty floor space. They are attractive when featured on pedestals and plant stands; raised to eye level, they also can act as indoor trees. This group includes an array of plants such as cast-iron plant, dieffenbachia, Chinese evergreen, rubber plant, and Swiss-cheese plant.

Tall treelike plants are another important part of an indoor landscape, and a few will go far thanks to their size and presence. This category includes banana, dracaena, figs such as *Ficus benjamina*, and tall palms.

Columnar plants are well placed in simple interiors. These plants tend to grow upright, without soft edges or draping effects. Rubber plants and various large cacti share this bold, upright look; sansevieria, with its tall, swordlike fronds, is another example.

Climbing and trailing plants, with their softening effect, are a finishing touch. Many climbers need a support such as a trellis, hooks, or hangers applied to a ceiling or wall. Trailing plants often have soft stems that cascade downward. In hanging baskets, the stems cover the pot itself, giving an even more interesting effect. There are many climbing and trailing plants from which to choose, including those that flower, such as strawberry begonia, orchid cactus, rat-tail cactus, goldfish plant, hoya, and lipstick plant. A number of foliage plants do an equally good job of lighting up an interior with their presence. These greenery plants include creeping fig, Swedish and grape ivy, trailing philodendron, pothos, spider plant, and wandering Jew.

The key to a vibrant indoor garden is healthy vegetation. So, what should you look for when you choose plants? There are a variety of considerations, and careful attention to detail will help you choose robust, vigorous specimens.

Take care when you obtain plants at nurseries or garden centers or when you receive them from direct merchants. A single plant harboring disease or infestations quickly can spread illness or pests to your other, healthy plants. Once a plant becomes ill, returning it to a healthy state is often a challenge. You will be better off from the start if you introduce only healthy plants to your indoor garden.

To choose a healthy plant, look for new growth that is firm, thriving, and normal in size, rather than small, distorted, shriveled, or overly soft, all of which are signs of fungal disease. The plant should be well shaped, with new growth. Avoid those with leggy growth, frequently a sign of having grown with sustained insufficient light. Choose a plant that is firmly anchored in the soil; wobbly plants that appear to be loosely rooted may have fungal diseases or damaged root systems. Look for fairly uniform color throughout the plant and robust, vibrant leaves. Droopy, wilted foliage on a plant rooted in wet soil usually means that it's suffering from a fungal or bacterial infection of its roots that prevents it from taking up water. Leaves also should be free of tip browning, an indication that the plant has been subjected to too-dry conditions.

Check carefully for signs of pests on the foliage's tops and bottoms, examining closely all plant cracks and crevices where pests such as mealybugs tend to be hidden. Look in the crown of the plant, in the leaf axils—located where the leaves meet the stem—and in new leaves that have yet to unfurl.

The root system of a plant is just as important as the foliage. You want abundant white, firm roots; if they're not pushing out of the bottom of the pot, remove the plant and take a quick look. Avoid plants whose roots are brown and soft, another sign of fungal or bacterial infection, and plants that are a mass of tangled, encircling roots.

When choosing plants, also heed your instincts. In general, if a plant is healthy, it's going to seem so. Such plants display an apparent vigor and frequently have a sheen to their green foliage.

Even if a plant appears to be healthy when you bring it home, it's a good idea to keep it isolated for 3 weeks, during which time you can monitor it for hidden pests and diseases.

SELECTING HEALTHY PLANTS

Start your search for a healthy houseplant in a well-maintained garden center (below). Flowering plants in peak condition often are available at florists, as are unusual tropicals (bottom).

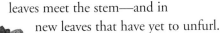

TOOLS AND MATERIALS

Although few basic tools are necessary for a bountiful indoor garden, having these essentials on hand will make your indoor gardening experience a good one. Start out with the following supplies, and then add others as your collection of plants and expertise grow and your care needs change.

You will need a small watering can with a capacity of 1–2 quarts (1.1–2.3 l) and a long, thin spout; broad spouts created for outdoor plants tend to splash too much water for indoor use. You also will require a larger watering can with a measuring scale for correctly measuring liquid fertilizer. If you intend to water hanging plants while they remain in place, a kitchen faucet and coiled-hose hookup will allow you to water high places with ease. Remember to check their soil periodically to avoid overwatering.

Some special equipment is required for trimming plants and propagating—growing new plants from existing ones. High-quality pruning shears, all-purpose gardening scissors, and a sharp knife are all necessities. You also will need rooting hormone, charcoal powder for disinfecting cuts, and a propagation soil mix. You can create your own mix by combining equal parts of horticultural sand, vermiculite, and peat moss. Plant markers are advisable so that you can note when you planted seed, propagated, or repotted a plant.

Perhaps most important is a supply of potting mixtures. Many plants do well with a high-quality potting soil; be sure that the one you choose contains a draining agent such as perlite or pumice. Some blooming plants need specialty potting mixes—orchid bark and African violet mix, for example. Add a large plastic pail for ease of mixing soils.

Obtain various pots in a variety of sizes and materials, depending on the size of your plants and the look you seek for your interior. If you will be raising seedlings, you'll also need a seedling tray. Those featuring removable lids are especially useful and help keep the humidity high, which many seeds require for germination. In addition to containers, drainage rocks, pea gravel, or stones are a must.

Fertilizer needs will depend on the type of plants you are growing. For most foliage houseplants, a general, all-purpose liquid organic plant food is best. If you will be growing flowering houseplants, such as African violets and orchids, you'll need fertilizer specifically formulated for them.

Stands, supports, and trellises are helpful for large or trailing plants. You'll find many types in nurseries and garden centers, or you can fashion your own supports and trellises from disease-free twigs and branches gathered from your garden. Use green garden tape to fasten plants onto supports; it stretches as a plant grows.

For low-light interiors, you also should consider a supplemental lighting system or special lights. To check humidity levels and air temperatures, a hygrometer and a thermometer are useful tools. Add a moisture meter for deciding when watering is needed—it's a handy extra.

To help detect a pest or disease infestation, keep on hand a 10x hand lens or a magnifying glass; for treatment, choose rubbing alcohol, insecticidal soap, and horticultural oil.

(Top) Houseplant supplies include a variety of general and specialty fertilizers, insecticidal soaps for controlling pests, and moisture-retentive sprays to help avoid brown leaf tips.

(Below) If your indoor garden is modest, consider diminutive hand tools such as claws, trowels, and pruning shears. For repotting larger plants, full-sized garden implements work best. Remember a pair of sharp scissors is effective for pruning houseplant foliage.

Once you start looking, you'll be delighted to find houseplants available just about everywhere. They're abundant at nurseries, garden centers, home centers, farmer's markets, and florists, as well as in the electronic marketplace and through specialty grower catalogs. Keep your ears and eyes open come springtime and you'll also likely hear about plant sales held by local public gardens and university arboretums. Such institutions often are experimenting and usually offer new, unusual, and sometimes rare plants.

Before acquiring any plant, it's prudent to carefully evaluate its source. Besides looking at the health and well-being of the plants [see Selecting Healthy Plants, pg. 21], examine the overall state of affairs in the retail establishment. Are display areas neat and tidy? Is it obvious that plants are receiving regular care? Does the plant supplier have knowledgeable staff eager to answer questions? Are plants clearly marked with both their common and scientific names, their planting instructions, and the care they should receive? What guarantee or return policy applies in case something goes awry or the plant doesn't thrive?

While the electronic marketplace and its accompanying information resources have opened up an exciting new world when it comes to collecting and growing houseplants, it's also important to seek advice appropriate to your particular geographic locale. Even indoors, temperature and humidity will vary somewhat between areas as diverse as Toronto, Charleston, and Las Vegas, creating factors that should influence plant choices in each locale. At times a certain species of a plant is more suited to a particular area. If the plant is a specialty item with specific humidity and temperature needs, it might be a good idea to learn more about its requirements. First try to obtain the plant through a local source with a track record of growing the plant successfully in your area; if local growers prove challenging to locate, turn to direct or electronic retailers, order the plant you need, and consider the process an adventure.

SOURCES AND RESOURCES

(Top) Many public gardens and arboretums offer surplus plants to visitors. They are an excellent source of accurate information on the growing and care of plants.

(Middle) Many garden centers and nurseries have knowledgeable staff to assist you and suggest plants for your home.

(Above) Electronic information resources are as close as your fingertips with data about rare and unusual plants.

(Left) When making selections, carefully note the light, humidity, and temperature conditions in each plant's display area.

INDOOR GARDENING FLOWCHART

A flowchart is a written checklist that allows you to quickly scan the major decisions that should be reviewed as you consider a garden project. Spend a few minutes with this chart to ensure that you remember each step to a successful indoor garden. It will save you time and effort, including unnecessary repeat trips to the garden store.

DETERMINING YOUR OBJECTIVES

1 **Goal and Planning Questions:** Will plants be the main feature in your home's rooms, or will they serve as a secondary decorative element? Will you grow plants primarily for their ability to enhance the look of your home, are you interested in the hobby aspect of growing plants, or will you grow plants for their blooms or fruit? Do you wish to use plants for visual appeal—to make rooms look larger or smaller—or to highlight and camouflage an architectural feature? How much time will you have to garden indoors? Can you care for houseplants with special requirements, moving large floor plants or accessing hanging planters? Who else lives in your home—for instance, are there young children or pets to consider?

SITE AND INDOOR CLIMATE

2 **Site Choice Questions:** What are the environmental conditions of the sites where you will add houseplants? How is the lighting? Is the room humid, or does it tend to be dry? Does the area have adequate air circulation and match the temperature range needs of the plants you want to grow? Should you acquire equipment to test for appropriate climatic conditions such as a hygrometer to measure relative humidity, a thermometer to check temperatures, and a moisture meter to check soil dampness? Can you modify areas lacking ideal conditions you require by providing additional warmth, humidity, or light? Will the plants you wish to grow fit in the room?

MATCHING ROOM DECOR

3 **Design and Fit Questions:** What is your decor style, and what sort of an ambience do you wish to create with houseplants? Do you prefer a tropical look, a traditional feel, or a more modern, austere look? Do you have a design theme you'd like to augment with houseplants? Should you choose houseplants with existing wall and window coverings in mind? Do you want to use plants to highlight furnishings, or will the plants become your focal point? Are foliage plants your main interest, or do you wish to add flowering houseplants to your decor? What sort of leaf shapes and textures would you like in your home—thin, pointy, lacy, wispy, large, variegated, broad, or straplike?

PREPARING TO SELECT HOUSEPLANTS

4 **Houseplant Selection Questions**: How much space do you have for houseplants? Are you interested in small, tabletop plants, or do you also desire climbers, large floor plants, and, hanging plants? What sort of conditions can you provide for the plants? How do you classify the lighting in your home, and does it vary from room to room? Is the florist, garden center, or nursery where you will obtain your plants orderly and well organized? Are staff members knowledgeable? Is their stock of plants well maintained, healthy, and free of pests? Do the plants have new growth? Do the plants seem healthy and vibrant?

MATERIALS AND RESOURCES

5 **Supplies and Care Questions**: What materials, supplies, tools, and soils will you need? Will you require special soil mixes and fertilizers? Are your pots the appropriate size for your plants? Do you have necessary materials for installing hanging plants, including hooks and hardware? Do you need any plant stands, trellises, or other supports? How will you water your houseplants—especially any out-of-the-way plants? To which common pests and diseases are your desired houseplants susceptible, and what preventive measures do you need to control them? Do you have a convenient workspace such as a potting table? Do you have an indoor sink suitable for deep watering plants?

FINDING HELP AND INFORMATION

6 **Experts and Aid Questions**: Where will you turn for expert advice? Have you consulted this book's encyclopedia of houseplants or other catalogs, periodicals, and books that contain information you will need? Does your garden store have knowledgeable staff able to answer your questions? Will you use online electronic resources for advice or contact your university, USDA, or an Agriculture Canada extension office agent? Are gardening classes available through local educational institutions? Are there experts who broadcast in radio or television media to whom you may turn with questions? Are there nearby public gardens and arboretums where you can obtain reliable information and plants?

Planning Indoor Gardens

Now that you've reviewed your options, it's time to start planning an indoor garden to suit your wishes and best meet your goals. Plants are lovely in their own right and will add to a home simply by their placement in a room. They'll be even more effective if you take time to choose plants that complement your furnishings and your wall and window coverings.

In this chapter, you'll discover how to match houseplants to your decor and use their fabulous forms, colors, leaf textures, and flowers to bring out the best in your home. By combining your decorating scheme and the natural aesthetic qualities of plants, you will create a stunning place to live.

So that you will be as successful with your indoor garden, you'll also learn how to determine what plants are right for your particular situation. A section on common houseplant groupings and their basic care requirements such as watering, fertilizing, light needs, as well as their preferences for temperature and humidity will help you match them to your environment and lifestyle.

You will explore sources and quality of light and learn how to tell if plants are receiving an adequate amount, with instructions for treating specific light conditions. You'll find more helpful information on humidity and air circulation, two important aspects of growing healthy houseplants. This chapter also takes a close look at tall and trailing plants, which often are the cornerstone of an eye-catching indoor garden.

You'll review a functional yet decorative aspect of growing houseplants—plant supports and stands. The proper stake will hold up a flowering plant or vine, keeping it shapely and healthy, while it adds an elegant or whimsical touch. You'll find information about various types of supports available and complete instructions for making your own from such garden cuttings as tree branches that you dry and cure before use. Finally, you'll learn what makes a good potting table, how you will benefit by acquiring one, and why you should consider obtaining one as your top priority.

Your reward for all the planning, will be healthy, attractive houseplants that meet all of your goals and fulfill your every dream.

A few thoughtful minutes spent perusing brochures and periodicals for ideas, sketching your home's rooms and considering how they naturally divide into environments will ensure your outcome will be both beautiful and healthy for the plants.

MATCHING DECOR

When it comes to decorating, it's the details that make the difference in really pulling a home together. Houseplants are among those essential elements. Most furnishings and architectural aspects involve hard surfaces and straight lines. Much like fabrics in the home, houseplants add softness and depth to a space; just like textiles, foliage comes in a stunning array of options from which to choose.

Take a look at plant foliage shapes, textures, and colors and you will be amazed at how easily you can match houseplants to your home's drapery and upholstery. There are many different leaf shapes, from the thin, pointy fronds of various palms to the elegant, dainty foliage of an asparagus fern, the fluffy, feathery look of a Boston fern, to the big, bold, colorful foliage of a bird-of-paradise. Textures also are wide ranging, from the smooth, shiny leaves of anthurium and rubber plant to the more feathery foliage

(Right) Match decorative elements and art to your houseplants to unify a room and establish a theme. Here, a framed painting of a Tuscan street and hanging geranium planters combine with a table plant to make a bold visual statement.

(Below) Choose wall coverings and decorative items that embody a floral theme, such as a fabric-covered bulletin board, wrought-iron frame, and note card set.

of the maidenhair fern. Some leaves are serrated, and there are even plants with foliage that resembles fabric, including the soft leaves of the aptly named purple velvet plant, coleus, and many begonias. Plants come in just about every color of the rainbow. You'll see shades of blue, green, pink, red, yellow—even near black—as well as myriad plants that have either variegated and patterned foliage in cream, red, white, and yellow.

Augment specific styles when choosing plants. For a southwest look, for instance, cacti, various succulents, and some dracaenas make great accompaniments. For a contemporary interior, use specimen orchids and plants with bold colors and straight lines such as sansevieria. For an even more unusual look, try a ponytail palm. Whatever you choose, make your home vibrant and unique by taking advantage of the wide array of plant foliage styles, colors and textures.

COMPLEMENTING INTERIOR DESIGN

1 At a nursery or garden store, judge plants by how their shape will fit with your furnishings: fan-shaped, columnar, mounded, spreading, or bushy.

As you begin your quest for a coordinated look, note these four aspects of your plants' future setting: form, pattern, texture, and color. Also consider wall and trim colors, window treatments, floor coverings, and fabric choices to help you choose plants that suit your room. Paint chips—available at home centers and paint retailers—are a convenient way to compare colors and remind you of textures and shapes as you select plants to match. Fill a clipboard with chips and notes, and follow these steps:

2 Note foliage similar to your existing fabric patterns and surface textures; choose from spearlike, feathery, fernlike, tropical, dense, or open-growth leaf patterns.

3 Consider the appearance of the foliage itself. On some plants it's solid, variegated, and fringed; on others it may be fuzzy, hairy, leathery, rough, smooth, or shiny.

4 If form, pattern, and texture suit your needs, select foliage colors to complement, match, or contrast with their future surroundings.

5 Choose planting containers suited to the selected plants, matching them to the color and decor found in your room.

UPKEEP AND CARE CHOICES

The type of plants you choose for your interior garden will determine the amount of time you will spend on upkeep and care. Some plants such as cacti and succulents need very little maintenance, while others—African violets and orchids, for instance—are more demanding. Before selecting plants for your indoor decor, examine the needs of various plants and then determine which ones are best for you. Carefully consider how much time you have for indoor gardening tasks such as watering, pinching, pruning—trimming—and fertilizing.

In terms of care requirements, plants fall into three categories—low, medium, and high maintenance. Plants in the low-maintenance group generally do well in most situations, even with low humidity, inconsistent watering, and spotty fertilizing. With the exception of cacti and succulents, most also can get by on low light, and pruning usually isn't required. Plants that fall into this category include a variety of easy-to-grow favorites such as aloe, billbergia, cactus, cast-iron plant, dieffenbachia, Chinese evergreen, pothos, and sansevieria.

Medium-maintenance plants usually require medium to bright light, regular watering and fertilizing, and in some cases additional humidity. Pruning sometimes is necessary. This group also is large and includes anthurium, croton, coleus, dracaenas, various ferns, ficus, ponytail and other palms, peace lily, peperomia, prayer plant, purple velvet plant, spider plant, umbrella tree, and zebra plant.

High-maintenance plants have narrow and specialized requirements in terms of light, humidity, watering, fertilizing, pruning, and even their potting medium. Many are flowering or fruiting plants that require constant, sometimes daily, attention. Plants that fall into this category include African violet, banana, begonia, citrus, fuchsia, and some of the orchids.

(Above) Limit your use of waxy leaf polishes, choosing instead those with mild soaps that help remove greasy cooking residues. Apply them sparingly, then rinse the plant's foliage with plenty of distilled or demineralized water.

(Right) When soil in a plant's pot starts to become compacted, install a water reservoir that slowly releases water such as the hollow, decorative squirrel seen in this container. Such aids are a temporary solution; repot the plant into fresh soil to remedy the condition.

HOUSEPLANT CARE REQUIREMENTS

Care Need	Requirements	Conditions
Light	Proper lighting is critical to plant health. Both intensity and duration of light are integral to plant growth. Plants require high, medium, or low light. Too much light or insufficient light will lead to plant challenges.	Indications of too much light: leaf drop, yellow leaves, wilting, brown or yellow spotting, flower bud drop. Indications of insufficient light: yellow leaves; leggy, spindly growth; failure to bloom; flower bud drop; less, smaller new growth; loss of variegated markings; and color on foliage.
Humidity	Most houseplants tend to favor humid conditions.	Indications of inadequate humidity: sluggish growth, yellowing leaves, brown leaf tips and margins, leaf curling, leaf drop, flower bud drop, dry brittle leaves. Indications of too much humidity: downy mildew.
Soil Fertility	Ideal soil for houseplants drains readily and provides airspace for plant roots yet is nutrient-rich and able to hold moisture. Soils low in fertility will lead to plant stress and challenges.	Indications of soil fertility inadequacies: rootbound plants, black leaf spot, soil compaction, salt buildup, improper drainage, incorrect pH levels, less and smaller new growth, soggy soil, and fungal disease.
Watering	Proper watering is critical to plant health. When and how you water will affect your plants, which rely on proper watering for survival. Too much or insufficient water can lead to plant disease or failure.	Indications of overwatering: brown leaf tips and margins; yellowing leaves; leaf drop; wilting, brown, or yellow leaf spotting; flower bud drop; soft stems; soggy soil; fungal disease; stem and crown or root rot. Indications of insufficient watering: brown leaf tips and margins; leaf drop; wilting, dry, brittle leaves; flower bud drop; rolled up leaves; less and smaller new growth.
Fertilizing	Plants require various minerals to manufacture their own food from sunlight and soil nutrients. Properly fed plants have lusher and thicker growth. Under- and overfeeding can lead to plant challenges.	Indications of underfertilizing: yellow leaves; iron chlorosis; less, smaller new growth; failure to bloom; flower bud drop. Indications of overfertilizing: brownish or black spots on leaf margins or tips, yellow leaves, leaf drop.
Temperature	In general, most houseplants do well in average home temperatures ranging from 65–75°F (18–24°C). Some sensitive plants, however, react to too-low or too-high temperatures and suffer in drafty locations. Some plants require a change in temperature to promote blooming—usually a cooler period in the winter months. Location in the home affects temperatures for plants. Window locations, for instance, can change temperatures drastically throughout the year.	Indications of temperatures that are too high: yellow leaves, wilting, failure to bloom, sun scorch. Indications of temperatures that are too low: leaf drop, brown or yellow spotting of leaves or stems, flower bud drop, pale spots on leaves.
Pruning	Some houseplants require regular pruning or pinching to remain shapely and healthy and to maintain vigor and strong appearance. Inadequate or improper pruning can cause plant challenges.	Indications of inadequate pruning: lanky, leggy growth; long gaps between leaves; dead growth; crossing stems; little or no flowering. Indications of overpruning: failure to bloom (flower buds removed during pruning), sparse appearance.

LIGHT SOURCES AND QUALITY

For proper growth, all green plants need some light. While specific requirements vary, foliage plants generally need less light than blooming or fruiting ones, and variegated foliage plants require more light than those with all-green leaves.

Both light intensity (the amount available) and duration (length of exposure) are integral to plant growth, and plants are broadly categorized according to their light requirements: high, medium, or low. Fortunately, you probably can find an area in your home for plants with different lighting needs.

First, consider orientation—the direction a window faces. An East-facing window is generally a good location for a plant that requires high light conditions. This area receives direct sun in the morning and bright light the remainder of the day. For plants that need the most light, such as succulents and cacti, a West-facing window is a good location. During most of the year, this window receives good light throughout the day, with direct sun in the afternoon. For plants that do best in bright but indirect light, a window that receives good light all day is ideal. The light will be strongest in front of the window; place plants that need medium light away from the window. Rooms with less exposure to the sun are best for plants that require low light levels. Light is medium in intensity right in front of these windows but drops off considerably once you move a distance away from them.

Next, consider light intensity and duration. Intensity can be affected by a variety of factors, including how clean the window is and your window coverings. Light coming through an uncovered window will be more intense than light shining through curtains, even those that are sheer. The amount of sun each window location receives—as well as the duration—varies, depending on the season. Watch carefully and note any light changes throughout the year.

When natural light is insufficient for the type of plants you want to grow, consider supplemental lighting. There are three main types of supplemental lighting from which to choose. These include fluorescent lighting, which comes in tubes and is installed in shop lights. Use full-spectrum fluorescent lights that simulate sunlight and place the plants 6–12 inches (15–30 cm) from the light.

(Top) Place plants based on their light needs. Areas range from bright- to low-light levels.

(Middle) Replace an under-cabinet fixture's tube with a fluorescent one with a full-light spectrum—often called a "grow light" or "plant light."

(Bottom) A greenhouse window in a kitchen is an ideal spot for a planter of light-loving herbs.

To provide plants with more usable light, try grow lights made with metal halide filaments. These can be screwed into standard electric light sockets, and since the light they emit is more intense, they can be placed up to 2 feet (60 cm) away from plants.

A third type of lighting—High Intensity Discharge Light Systems, or HID—traditionally has been used by commercial greenhouses. These lights duplicate the type of light the sun emits; you can use them to grow just about anything indoors, including tropicals, fruits, and vegetables. HID systems include a bulb, ballast, and reflector, draw lots of current, and produce substantial amounts of heat. You will find HID lighting through the electronic marketplace and at some specialty nurseries or lighting stores.

EVALUATING LIGHT IN A SITE

1 Place plants that require high light in a spot near an area with many windows that receive bright sun throughout the day. Use only neutral-colored, sheer curtains to diffuse the sun's direct rays.

Plants vary in their need for light according to their area of leaf surface and amount of chlorophyll. Some plants have adapted to strong light conditions, others to partial or total shade. Three broad classes describe these plant light requirements—high, medium, and low. Match your plants to your location by following these steps:

2 Add more light in marginal areas by placing plants near a white or light-colored wall that will reflect light.

3 For medium-light plants, add vertical or horizontal blinds to filter direct sunlight that falls near a window.

4 East- and West-facing windows naturally receive about one-third the total sunlight of windows that face the noonday sun. With little or no window coverings, they are ideal for medium-light plants.

5 Room centers, corners opposite windows, and areas shaded by solid furnishings are suitable for plants with low-light needs.

6 If necessary, add full-spectrum plant lights—so-called grow lights—to boost the amount of light available for the plants.

HUMIDITY AND AIR CIRCULATION

Many popular houseplants originated in tropical settings, where the air is heavy with humidity; such conditions seldom are found in most homes outside the tropics. Although many of these tropical descendants do survive in low-humidity areas, most perform much better with a little extra moisture. A few truly need high humidity to survive. Plants challenged by low atmospheric humidity will have sluggish growth, yellowing leaves or brown tips, and leaf curling. Flowers buds will form but dry up without opening.

Most plants require at least 40 percent humidity. Test the moisture level in your home with a hygrometer, an instrument available in most hardware stores that measures relative humidity. If you need to raise the humidity—often just a few percentage points can make the difference—you can use one or more techniques to do so, depending on how much of a change you require. After you have taken steps to raise the humidity level, retest it with the hygrometer to see if you've reached your goal.

One effective solution to low moisture levels is a humidity tray. Fill a waterproof plate or bowl with polished stones, pebbles, or marbles, and add water, stopping when the water level is just below the surface of the stones. Place the plant on top, making sure that no water touches the bottom of the pot. Or, if you prefer, double pot your plant and fill the space in between with sphagnum moss; spray the moss on a regular basis to keep it moist.

Grouping plants creates a more humid environment for them because water transpires from plant leaves. The more plants you put together, the more humidity they create for one another. Mulching with moss or stones raises the humidity level, too.

You also can set plants near an indoor fountain or run a humidifier. Adjust heating system humidifiers to 60 percent. Place plants that require extremely high humidity in a terrarium, where humidity runs 80–100 percent.

Air circulation is another important consideration. Plants need fresh air for many reasons, chiefly to prevent disease and insect infestation. In many cases, sufficient air movement is created when temperatures drop at night, when people walk past plants, or when doors open and shut. If you suspect stagnant air is a problem for your plants, especially those located in corners and bunched together—tip-offs are insect and fungal conditions—consider ventilating the room with a ceiling fan or small tabletop fan pointed away from the plants. If air blows directly on the plants. the leaves will dry out. Similarly, place plants away from heater or air-conditioning ducts and open windows only during periods of mild weather.

Natural circulation flows in a pattern that carry air up or down a room's outside walls. Plants in these locations receive more air than do those in central room locations. An open fireplace flue also will provide breezes to your plants—keep in mind they should be moved if you light a fire in the fireplace.

CHOOSING A LOCATION

Vents from heating, ventilating, and air-conditioning distribute heated or cooled, low-humidity air that can overheat, chill, or dehydrate indoor plants. Direct sunlight also can overheat plants, burning their leaves or drying their soil. Choose the right location for your plants, following these steps:

1 Measure the distance traveled by drafts from heater vents by using a helium-filled balloon tied to a weighted string. Mark the draft-free areas.

2 During winter heating months and summer air-conditioning months, check the humidity in your room, using an electronic hygrometer.

3 Use an ultrasonic water vaporizer to quickly increase the humidity within your home. Indoor fountains also supply moisture.

4 Room dividers can block air circulation; use small desk or ceiling fans to keep the air moving around plants.

5 Pick locations where plant containers are shaded from direct sunlight. For tropicals that require high humidity, set the plant on rocks in a tray partially filled with water.

6 Place plants with similar needs into group arrangements. Each of the plants releases moisture, keeping the humidity level up.

TALL AND TRAILING PLANTS

You may wish to complete your indoor garden with tall floor plants, which add a dramatic look to a room, and trailing plants, which can trail the length of a room at ceiling height or drape from high above. Verticality is important in the indoor garden; it invites the eye up, creates interest and contrast, and provides a feeling of being surrounded by greenery.

Big floor plants make their presence felt simply with their height and bulk. Use them to soften the effect of a room, fill in empty corners, and camouflage areas. Although big plants generally look best in large rooms, floor plants also can be used in smaller rooms when they're properly located. Place them in corners or where you otherwise would put furniture.

Trailing plants give a room the same kind of finished look as window coverings. As a matter of fact, they make a good window frame as well as a terrific wallpaper border when they're trained to grow around the expanse of a room. Let vining and trailing plants gracefully spill from lofty heights such as bookcases and lofts, or train them to cover a wall.

Use tall floor plants as well as those that trail below a hanging pot or ledge to soften featureless walls and help create a point of visual focus in a room's corner.

When it comes to watering elevated plants, you have several options. If you can, remove plants from high locations on a regular basis, water them over the sink, and allow them to drain well before you return them to their site. Alternatively, you can considerably reduce the time necessary for watering by using self-watering pots, which have built-in water reservoirs that provide water through capillary action to plants as needed. A hanging-plant waterer is simply a squeeze bottle with a long nozzle with a hooked end at its tip. You compress the bottle, and the water travels up the tube and releases into the plant. Or you can acquire a coiled, retractable hose that attaches to a kitchen or utility sink. Whichever watering method you choose, you should still take the plant down periodically and check that you're not over- or underwatering. Also keep in mind that plants at high elevations are subject to warmer temperatures and tend to dry out easily, so more frequent misting may be necessary in mountain regions.

Large floor plants are easy to reach, but because of their size they usually need to be watered in place. Let water run out the bottom of the pot into the saucer, then promptly remove any excess—a turkey baster works well—to avoid having the roots stand in water.

FITTING PLANTS TO SPACE

1 Measure the vertical height of the wall or area behind the plant's location, then divide it in thirds. Here, one-third the height of an 8-ft. (2.4-m) wall is 32 in. (80 cm), and two-thirds is 64 in. (1.6 m).

Fitting houseplants to locations within your home is simple when you use the designer's rule of thirds—the vertical space the plant occupies should be either one-third or two-thirds of the visual area of its surroundings. For best appearance, plants with heights about 1.5 times greater or smaller than their widths fit another rule—the golden rectangle. Learn how to use these two easy concepts with houseplants, following these steps:

3 For tabletop plants, measure the table's width or length, and use a third of that measurement to select plants that fit the area.

2 Plants with heights equal to either calculated height will appear more pleasing in the space than either shorter or taller plants.

4 Position plants by dividing surface into thirds in both directions. Intersections of these divisions are the best spots to display the plants.

5 Choose houseplants 1.5 times wider than tall or taller than wide. These proportions mimic those found in many architectural settings.

6 Use adjustable plant stands to add extra height and added beauty, or to allow for growth.

SUPPORTS AND STANDS

Staking a plant, or tying it to a post or wooden pole, may serve several functions. It helps an unsteady plant stand up straight, holds up the long, flowering stems of plants such as orchids so they are displayed to their best advantage, and enables gardeners to train climbing plants to grow in a particular direction.

Staking and training also offer you a decorating opportunity. You can obtain decorative supports through nurseries and home supply stores, or you can create your own from disease-free twigs and branches. Commercially available stakes and supports come in a variety of styles and generally are made of metal, bamboo, or wood. They usually are green, brown, tan, or black. You'll find everything from single stakes to decorative plant towers and heart-shaped topiary frames.

If you wish to fashion your own supports and stakes from materials in your garden, you will need new cuttings that remain fairly pliable. Some flexible plants such as willow tend to work better than others for this purpose, and you might wish to experiment. Shape them as you wish, tying them securely with aluminum wire plant ties. They will keep their new shape after they dry.

Plant stands enable you to elevate and highlight certain plants in your indoor garden. A well-designed stand gives a plant height and also is a great spot for trailing and climbing plants. A peace lily sitting on a table always is impressive; place it atop a plant stand and it becomes the focal point of a room. Likewise, a lipstick plant may look good hanging up high, but it also can be especially striking placed on a plant stand at eye level.

A wide variety of plant stands are available, making it possible to choose one that complements your decor. You'll find metal stands, those with ceramic tops, and wooden or wicker stands. Many are multilayered, so you can show off an array of plants.

The best plant stands are made of waterproof materials and have sinklike top shelves that hold the plants in a basin immune to water draining from the plants, although those that are purely decorative are suited to many uses.

Antique stepladders make excellent multilevel stands on which to display collections of bric-a-brac and your houseplants. Here, a Boston fern, begonia, and other plants mingle with items in a seashore theme.

POTTING TABLES

Your work space is important. While potting up, inspecting, and pruning your houseplants is performed conveniently on a kitchen table or counter, a good potting table makes indoor gardening more enjoyable. When you have all of your tools and materials close at hand you can quickly and easily perform gardening tasks. You'll find that a well-designed model—one with abundant surface area, convenient shelves, and numerous drawers—allows you to quickly repot a plant or treat it for pests and diseases.

A wide variety of potting tables with various dimensions are available, or you can build your own. When choosing a work space, consider the height you find most comfortable. If you will be gardening from a sitting position, plan for that as well.

BUILDING A MODULAR PLANT STAND

Required Materials:

From ½-in. (13-mm) particle board:

1	24⁹⁄₁₆×30-in. (62.4×76-cm)	Side panel stock
1	8×24-in. (20×61-cm)	Top shelf
1	11×24-in. (28×61-cm)	Middle shelf
1	14×24-in. (35.5×61-cm)	Bottom shelf
2	2×29½-in. (5×75-cm)	Retainer bars
1	20×30-in. (51×76-mm)	Back panel
9	5d	Finishing nails
1	qt (1 l) Latex exterior gloss paint	

Build this attractive plant stand that disassembles easily for flat storage. It can be made of economical particle board or plywood, and painted with latex exterior paint, following these easy steps:

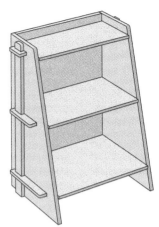

1 Cut stock to measure. Mark points 16 in. (40.6 cm) along the 24⁹⁄₁₆-in. (62.4-cm) length of the side panel stock from two opposing diagonal corners, connect them, and cut the diagonal.

2 Refer to the diagram. Carefully mark each cut. Drill holes in each mortise with a hand drill fitted with a ⁹⁄₁₆-in. (14-mm) spade bit. Cut mortises and tenons with a jigsaw.

3 Use a jigsaw or sander to round the top front corners of the two side panels, both edges of each shelf tenon, and the top corners of the retainer bars.

4 Lay the side panels face down on their diagonal edges. Fit each shelf tenon into its mortise, adjusting as needed. Avoid forcing if the fit is too snug. Slide the retainer bars into the mortises in the shelves.

5 Fit the back panel between and flush with the side panels. Square the assembly, drill three holes through the back panel into each shelf using a hand drill fitted with a ¹⁄₁₆-in. (1.5-mm) bit, and fasten the back panel with finish nails.

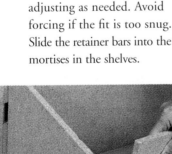

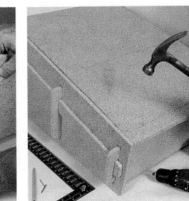

Now that you've decided what you want and have your plants, it's time to roll up your sleeves, pick up your trowel, and pot up your plants! If plants are new, however, wait for a few weeks before you begin. It's generally a good idea to let your plants acclimate to their new home for as long as a month before repotting them. It's also important to pot up a plant only if it needs it, as planting in a container that is too big can cause soil surrounding the roots to remain overly wet, a condition that often leads to fungal disease.

Planting using the right techniques, selecting and preparing the proper containers, choosing the best planting medium, and getting your new plantings off to a great start is the secret to success in your indoor garden of houseplants. Even if you already have a table full of foliage or flowering plants, take time to review the basics of planting and transplanting.

The following pages will guide you in the preparations necessary before you actually pot your plants. You'll learn how to choose containers and sterilize them to avoid transmitting disease between your plants. You'll also see how to provide plants with proper drainage and choose soil. A general-purpose soil works for many plants, but there are exceptions. Certain specialty plants such as cacti need a special mix, which you can prepare yourself. Others such as the epiphytes and orchids are best planted in soilless containers filled with bark chips. You'll find that matching the proper soil to your plants is the second step to take after choosing and preparing the right container.

Then, after taking you step-by-step through the planting procedure, this chapter offers tips for creating a kitchen herb garden and a mixed planting of several plants in a single container. You'll also examine the ins and outs of hanging plants and learn how to train bonsai and topiary. Finally, you'll discover how easy it is to bring the colorful, often fragrant presence of spring bulbs such as paperwhites into your home.

Whether your indoor gardening goals are modest or elaborate, you'll find out how to achieve them by planting with the right techniques and materials.

Start off right by preparing your containers, potting your plants, and installing them in your home

Planting in Containers

A potting table is the most convenient location for potting your indoor houseplants. It will hold your tools and all the materials you'll use to plant, has ample work space on its top, and is easily cleaned after use.

PREPARING CONTAINERS FOR PLANTING

Finding the right container for your plant is akin to discovering the right home for you and your family. Given the perfect pot, a plant is likely to grow and flourish for a long time. Like a house, though, a container needs a few finishing touches to make it a suitable home.

You can stick with traditional pots or use found objects to house your plants. An antique vase, pitcher, cookie jar, wicker basket, even an old washtub can make a lovely container. Be sure that whatever kind of container you choose—whether conventional or whimsical—has what it takes to grow a healthy plant.

A good container serves a variety of important purposes. It provides a decorative home for your houseplant; it also supplies a place where plant roots are insulated from heat and cold, where it can grow easily and thrive. This means choosing a pot that first and foremost has drainage holes. If you want to use a pot that lacks adequate drainage holes, use it as a cachepot—a holding pot—or drill holes yourself, using an electric drill fitted with a ½-inch (12-mm) masonry bit for terra-cotta and ceramic pots, or a carbide bit for plastic and metal containers [see Preparing Containers, pg. 45]. It's also a good idea to add extra holes if a pot is equipped with only a single, small opening.

Besides ensuring that a pot has adequate drainage, you should be certain that all pots are clean. Even brand-new containers made of synthetic material need to be washed to rid them of any cleaning solvents or other residue they may hold from the manufacturing process. Use liquid detergent and a scrub brush. If you want to place a plant in a pot that's been used before, plan to sterilize it first to kill any fungus spores or latent bacteria that could infect new plants [see Sterilizing Terra-Cotta Containers, opposite pg.].

The essentials you'll need for healthy houseplants include gloves, pots in a choice of sizes, paintable latex sealant, paintbrush, sterilizing solution made of household chlorine bleach, pebbles, and a cordless drill mounted with a masonry bit for drilling drain holes.

Further preparation of a pot will depend on the material of the container you select and the variety of plant it will hold. Clay and terra-cotta pots are an option for many plants. Keep in mind, however, that they are porous and water has a tendency to pass through them, leaching nutrients and depositing a scale-like film of soil salts on the exterior of the pot. Avoid them for plants that should stay continuously moist, or apply a breathable yet waterproof latex sealant to the container's interior before you plant in it [see Preparing Containers, pg. 45]. For best results, paint on two coats.

These few preplanting steps will help ensure your houseplants get off to a strong, healthy start. They'll reward your efforts with lush growth, beautifying your interior for years to come.

STERILIZING TERRA-COTTA CONTAINERS

I t makes economic sense and conserves resources to reuse pots for new plants as you repot others into larger ones [see Repotting Crowded Plants, pg. 80]. Before beginning, sterilize all your containers to prevent infection by fungal or bacterial diseases. Gather your pots, two plastic tubs, dishwashing soap, household bleach, and rubber gloves, then follow these steps:

1 Don gloves and mix a solution of 9 parts water to 1 part household bleach. Pour the solution into a plastic washtub.

2 Thoroughly wash each pot in soapy water to remove any clinging soil, rinse in ample plain water, and set aside to drain.

3 Soak each pot in the bleach sterilizing solution for at least 30 seconds, then remove, drain, and allow it to completely dry.

4 Always dispose of unused bleach solution safely. Pour it down a household drain, then flush with water.

Warning

Household bleach contains sodium hypo-chlorite, a powerful skin and eye irritant. Avoid hazard by wearing gloves and protective clothing whenever mixing or pouring bleach.

PROPER DRAINAGE

Good drainage is essential to plant health. Most houseplants will suffocate or develop fungal disease if they are left standing in water or their soil remains continuously wet. Regardless of the type of plant you grow, its pot must have adequate drainage holes.

Generally, it's best if a pot has more than one drainage hole so the water will penetrate the rootball and drain quickly. In addition, a single hole can become partially plugged at some point and cause water to collect at the base of the plant. With several drainage holes, soil also successfully leaches out excess salts.

Check pots regularly to make sure that they are draining freely. If a plant looks droopy yet the soil is damp, you've probably overwatered or the drain holes have become clogged with soil or roots [see Watering Houseplants, pg. 68].

If you use pots without drainage holes as cachepots, remember always to empty standing water from them after irrigation. You also should protect your plants against excessive moisture standing around their roots by placing the plant pot on an inverted saucer, pot, pebbles, or marbles set inside the cachepot. These risers will help keep the roots free of standing water and expose them to air—two conditions that are good for plants. As a matter of fact, some plants thrive when they're elevated over a water reservoir, because it increases humidity [see Humidity and Air Circulation, pg. 34].

Containers with true drainage holes are far superior to drainless pots, even when the latter are equipped with layers of stones or sand at their bottoms to give excess water somewhere to settle. In practice, the water in a closed pot actually wicks and pools above the stones or sand, creating overly wet roots likely to suffocate your plants or cause them to succumb to fungal disease.

Excess moisture also can be an issue with self-watering pots. While they reduce the amount of time spent watering, the soil in them stays wet for long periods, creating less-than-ideal conditions for most houseplants. For this reason, self-watering pots are best used only for plants that remain healthy when they are kept continually moist.

Regardless of the type of pot you choose, its a good idea to check the soil moisture each time you water the plant. If it remains moist to the touch, wait to water until the soil's surface has dried [see Watering Houseplants, pg. 68]. If a container that previously has drained adequately becomes slow to drain and develops standing water, check to see if its drain hole has become clogged; if so, free it of roots or other blockage if necessary.

Protect the drain hole of your pots from blockage by lining the bottom with coarse or medium pebbles, pottery shards, or other loose material. Containers with several drains are better than those with a single hole.

PREPARING CONTAINERS

The best planting containers have large, unobstructed drain holes. Sometimes, pots have small drain holes or lack them completely. If so, it's easy to drill a hole in most pots. Containers made of porous materials, such as terra cotta, should be sealed before they are used as planting pots. For drilling, you'll need eye protection and a power drill equipped with a special bit. For sealing, gather rubber gloves, a paint brush, and breathable latex sealant, available at most paint retailers and home centers. Follow these steps:

Drilling Drain Holes

1 Fit a power drill with a ½-in. (12-mm) bit. Use a carbide bit for iron and brass containers, a masonry bit for ceramic or concrete pots.

2 Apply crossed strips of masking tape to the pot's base, then mark its center point.

3 Drill the hole, allowing the bit to work its way into the pot's surface. Avoid applying too much pressure, which builds up frictional heat.

Applying Sealants

1 Prepare the container by washing and draining it. Allow it to thoroughly dry before you begin to apply sealant.

2 Don gloves, then paint an even layer of latex sealant on the container's inside surface. Allow it to dry.

3 Apply a second coat of latex sealant to the pot's interior. Allow it to dry for 24 hours before planting.

SOILS FOR PLANTING

Of all the components of indoor gardening, potting soil is the most important. Most plants need soil to hold them securely in place and provide them a location to grow roots. The more beneficial the holding material, the healthier the root system you will get and the heartier plants you will grow. Plant roots require several things of the soil. They need a soil that provides moisture, air, and nutrients. The mixture you choose must provide all of these things.

Most houseplants grow best in rich, well-drained soil with pumice or perlite as a draining agent. For plants that do best in always-moist conditions, choose soils that contain water-retaining polymers. When wet, these hard, clear granules expand into a gellike masses that hold water. As the soil dries, the polymers release water and keep the soil moist, extending the time between waterings.

Different suppliers of potting soil use different formulations, so always carefully examine the package contents as you consider your particular plants' needs. Some houseplants require their own special mix, such as African violets and other flowering plants, bromeliads, cacti, ferns, and epiphytes. Flowering plants generally do best in a mix containing organic water-holding materials such as shredded bark, compost, or peat moss. Such mixtures keep flowers and buds constantly moist and prevent bud drop. Water-retaining polymers also are good additions to such soil. Orchids, though, are in a different class when it comes to their potting mix. Because they are epiphytic, naturally growing on other plants for support with their roots exposed to the air rather than in soil, cultivate them in orchid bark instead of traditional potting soil; such mixes comprise a coarse blend of chips, often fir or pine bark. The bark supports the orchids, holding them upright, and allows plenty of air to get to their roots. Cacti also have their own special requirements. [see Soil for Cacti, this pg.].

In addition to a soil's water-retention properties, its degree of acidity and alkalinity—soil pH—is important. Most houseplants do best in slightly acidic soil. A few plants, however, prefer soil that is even more acidic, including azalea, citrus, and a number of ferns. For these, use a prepared azalea and camellia soil mix.

Keep in mind that, although your houseplant mix starts out acidic, it will change over time. You may have a very alkaline water supply—typically found throughout areas of the U.S. such as the desert southwest, the deep south, and Florida—in which case your soil's pH balance will change over time. Fertilizers also can cause soil to become more alkaline. If a plant begins to produce stunted, weak growth despite proper care, check the pH of its soil with a test kit or a meter. Soil with 6.5 pH or higher should be partially or totally replaced by repotting the plant, unless the plant it contains happens to be suited to higher pH.

SOIL FOR CACTI

As desert plants, cacti require a quite different soil mix than the average houseplant. As a matter of fact, cactus planted in a standard mix soon would become diseased from too much moisture. An effective cactus mix mimics the environmental conditions found in the desert, including fast drainage and high alkalinity. Cactus mixes are available prepackaged, but many enthusiasts prefer to mix their own. Here is a mix you can create for successful cactus growing:

- 2 parts compost or rich topsoil
- 1 part coarse sand
- 1 part calcined clay or ¼-inch (6-mm) lava pebble (to create excellent drainage similar to that found in the desert soils).

To 4 quarts (4.5 l) of mix, add 2 tablespoons (30 ml) dolomitic lime to create a more alkaline soil and ⅓ cup (80 ml) charcoal to sweeten the soil and reduce odor.

Soils and mediums for planting houseplants vary widely because each plant has specific needs. Some houseplants perform best when planted in soilless mixtures, while others require highly fertile soil rich in organics. You always should match the soil to your plant's particular requirements.

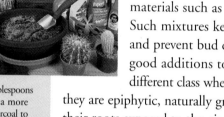

CONTAINER PLANTING

Most houseplants are perennials with extensive root systems that require protection and care as you transplant them from nursery containers into your pots. Always choose a pot that is at least one-third larger than the original container, check that it has adequate drainage holes or drill them yourself, then follow these steps:

1 Cover the container's drain hole with plastic mesh and pea gravel. Fill the container with moist potting soil, adding enough to reach 1–2 in. (25–50 cm) below the rim.

2 Ease your plant out of its nursery container and gently loosen the soil around the rootball with a hand fork. Cut any encircling roots.

3 With a hand trowel, dig a planting hole large enough for the plant's rootball. Set the plant into the soil, matching its depth to that of the nursery container.

4 Backfill and compact the soil using your fingertips or palms. Add more soil if necessary.

5 Water immediately after planting, applying foliar fertilizer at half its package-recommended strength. Allow the container to drain.

PLANTING TREES IN CONTAINERS

Planting Full-Size Trees

1 Cover the pot's drain holes with plastic mesh and pea gravel, then add a layer of potting soil, at least 3 in. (75 mm) deep.

Trees and shrubs—full-size and dwarf varieties—can be planted into pots large enough to accommodate their root systems and provide good drainage. Choose a container at least twice the size of the nursery container's width and depth, then follow these steps:

2 Lay the tree on its side, then pull gently, removing it from the nursery container. Cut any encircling roots. Set the rootball in the pot's center.

3 Fill around the rootball with potting soil, tamping it to compact it. Water the tree thoroughly, then apply foliar fertilizer at half the package-recommended strength.

Bonsai Miniatures

1 Place a layer of pea gravel, 1 in. (25 mm) deep, in a container with an Asian theme. Mound soil at its center, 3 in. (75 mm) deep. Set a picturesque rock atop the mound.

2 Remove the dwarf tree from its container. Use a gentle stream of water to wash away soil from around its roots.

3 Fan the roots over the rock and mound. Fill the container with soil, tamping it to compact it. Water the planting thoroughly.

GROW A KITCHEN HERB GARDEN

Add spice to your meals and spruce up your kitchen with practical greenery—herbs. Raise warm-climate herbs in a greenhouse window or a spot with direct, bright sunlight and grow moisture-loving herbs in indirect light. Naturals for your kitchen include basil, chives, mint, parsley, rosemary, sage, and thyme. To plant your herb garden, follow the general directions for planting [see Planting in Containers, pg. 47]. Gather a waterproof catch basin, decorative containers, plastic mesh, potting soil, a hand trowel, and your herbs, then follow these easy instructions:

1 Set your waterproof catch basin into the greenhouse window or atop a plant stand situated in a sunny spot.

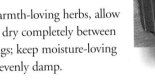

2 Plant your herbs, water them thoroughly, and allow them to drain. Arrange shortest species nearest the light, taller plants behind them.

3 Locate moisture-loving plants such as chervil, chives, and mint in partial shade.

4 For warmth-loving herbs, allow soil to dry completely between soakings; keep moisture-loving herbs evenly damp.

5 Rotate each of the plants a quarter turn every few days to promote even growth.

6 Every 2 weeks, apply liquid organic plant food diluted to half its recommended strength. Water herbs thoroughly after each fertilizer application.

MIXED PLANTINGS INDOORS

Mixed plantings give you a chance to create your own indoor miniature gardens. Group a number of different plants and you can make an instant decorative display with contrasting or complementary foliage types or colorful flowers. A basket brimming with red-toned plants such as begonia, coleus, croton, and *Dracaena tricolor*, for instance, looks stunning on a coffee table next to a green and red fabric sofa.

Mixed plantings often are created in baskets, but you also can use larger pots or planter boxes. Pot all the plants in the same container or fill a basket with several pots and cover them with sphagnum moss. If you use a single container, be sure all the plants have the same growing requirements [see Encyclopedia of Common Houseplants, pg. 87]. It's best to choose plants that do well in moist conditions; when grouped together, they create a humid environment as water transpires from their leaves.

(Right) The best mixed plantings include both upright and low or trailing plants to create interesting visual profiles.

(Below) If you use baskets lined with waterproof plastic to hold your mixed plantings, keep in mind the need to drain excess water from them to keep your plants healthy.

Choose plants of varying heights for your plant basket. In the center, place your tall plants, such as small dracaenas and palms, and surround them in descending order of height with other, lower-growing plants such as aluminum plant, coleus, and mosaic plant. Plant trailing and hanging plants on the edge of the container so they gracefully drape. Good choices include ivy, pothos, and spider plant. It's also a good idea to line the basket with plastic to prevent moisture from warping it or transmitting disease to your plants.

Care for your mixed-plant basket as you would any other houseplant. If the plants are in individual containers, remember to regularly remove them, and water and feed each plant according to its particular needs. If they are planted as a group, you should install slow-release watering reservoirs in the rootballs of any moisture-loving plants.

MIXING PLANTS
IN A CONTAINER

1 Prepare the container by covering its drain hole with pea gravel and partially filling the pot with potting soil.

Mixing houseplants with similar care needs allows you to make containers with contrasting foliage and varied heights. For best results, choose a large, deep container. Next, select a single tall species to feature and provide an anchor for the display. Pick between one and three plants that contrast with the main species. Gather the plants, pea gravel, potting soil, and a hand trowel, then follow these steps:

2 To display pots against a wall, set the main plant against a sidewall of the pot; otherwise, position it in the container's center.

3 At points angled 45° from the main plant's center, place two or three midsized species. Add potting soil to make them level with the main plant.

4 Fill space between plants with small or trailing species. Crowd them in, match the other plants' soil level, and compact their roots.

6 Thoroughly water the planting, allow it to drain, then place it in its display site.

5 Fill between the plants with more potting soil, compacting it with your fingertips.

HANGING PLANTS

Houseplants placed overhead can give height and visual interest to a room, enhance windows, and add a vertical complement to otherwise featureless corner spaces. Plants that droop, trail, creep, or climb are perfect candidates for hanging baskets or placement on other high perches. You can choose from plenty of attractive hanging plants, including green and variegated foliage plants such as strawberry begonia, ferns, ivy, wandering Jew, trailing philodendron, pilea, and spider plant, and those with blooms such as goldfish plant, hoya, and lipstick plant.

Because hanging plants frequently are quite heavy, it's important to carefully consider their location. Avoid installing them in traffic corridors, where they might pose a hazard to passersby. Also consider hanging plants at eye level, which makes them visible and their care easier. Install their hook and basket to a secure anchor, and check it for safety. Generally, plastic baskets are best for indoor growing; wire baskets filled with moss tend to be heavy and they can drip. They also are prone to dry out more quickly and need more frequent watering to thrive.

You can hang a basket with a single plant—a lipstick plant in full bloom is beautiful—or you can mix several plants in one big basket. For mixed plantings, coordinate a variety of leaf colors, textures, and hanging habits for an eye-catching arrangement. Asparagus fern, ivy, spider plant, and wandering Jew, for instance, create an interesting display. Experiment to find a look that appeals to you.

(Above) A decorative hook attached to a molly bolt can be installed quickly through wallboard ceilings but is designed to carry only limited weight.

(Right) Wall sconce brackets, which can be found at many hardware stores, are good for hanging small houseplants.

(Below) Columns and other risers are another way to position plants high overhead.

Keep in mind that hanging plants are exposed to more heat, lose water more quickly, and need more frequent watering than plants grown at or near floor level. While there are gadgets available for watering elevated plants, it's often best to remove a plant from its hanger and soak it—pot and all—in a bucket or sink full of water. Soak the plant for 15–20 minutes, or until all the bubbling stops, then allow it to thoroughly drain before returning it to its hanger or ledge for display.

To maintain the pleasing form of hanging houseplants, prune them regularly. Pruning frequency varies, and some plants grow more quickly than others. Note where growth has become unruly or out of proportion to the rest of the plant. Before pruning, step back and view the plant from various vantage points around the room, and then make your cuts. Remember to wash your pruners before and after use to keep you plants healthy.

INSTALLING SUPPORTS FOR HANGING PLANTS

A hanging plant with soil, water, and container may be heavy and always requires sturdy support. Gather an electronic stud finder, power drill, drill bits, hammer, an expansion anchor fitting with a hooked bolt, and a screwdriver, and follow these steps:

1 Use a stud finder to locate the center of a ceiling joist, carefully marking its location. It will support your hanger hook.

2 Mount a ⅛-in. (3-mm) wood bit into your electric drill. Drill a hole upward, vertically through the drywall and into the wooden joist.

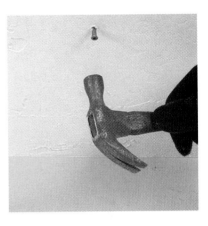

3 Use a hammer to drive the expansion anchor fitting into the hole. It should fit snugly.

4 Mount the hook bolt into the expansion fitting, then use a screwdriver to seat the bolt. The expansion fitting will widen as the bolt's threads tighten, gripping the wood.

5 Hang your plant by attaching its hardware or chain to the installed anchor.

SHAPING BONSAI AND TOPIARY

Bonsai—the craft of growing carefully trained, dwarfed trees or shrubs in small containers —is a unique blend of horticulture and art. In order to develop what appears to be a natural look and keep proportion in these miniature landscapes, plants require regular foliage and root pruning and frequent shaping of their young branches. Creating the windswept look of a Mughu pine involves a variety of techniques, including root binding and branch training with stout wire.

Although bonsai usually is linked with Japan and the term itself is Japanese, historians believe that the craft actually originated in China. The Japanese are believed to have adopted the art form in the 8th century. Since then, the rules and methods for bonsai have evolved. Today, Japan has entire nurseries dedicated to this plant form. Slow-growing species of pines and bamboos are popular subjects, as are many flowering trees and shrubs.

Indoor bonsai growing is a relatively new idea. Plants used for indoor bonsai are different from those grown outdoors. In general, plants that do well as indoor bonsai are woody and come from the Mediterranean region, the subtropics, and the tropics. Some—the ficus species, fuchsia, and *Murraya paniculata*, among them—are known as traditional houseplants.

Topiary is a related form of plant art, employing decorative shapes fashioned out of plants. Egyptians and Romans created topiaries, which were an integral feature of ancient gardens. Rosemary and ivy hoops and hearts are common indoor topiary subjects. You also can find topiary in a variety of animal shapes such as rabbits, swans, and bears. As is the case for bonsai, topiaries need regular pruning so they keep their desired shape. Training—directing the plant around and through the frame—also is necessary.

You can create your own topiary simply by sculpting wire into the shape of your geometric or animal subject. Keep in mind that topiaries often need time to fill in and take shape, usually 6 months to a year, depending on the support frame and the type of plant.

(Right) Through careful and regular pruning, this ivy will maintain its form. The plant's lower half is being trained down to grow over the pot.

(Below) Use sharp, small pruning shears to shape a topiary planting such as this miniature juniper.

PRUNING AND TRAINING GROWTH

Bonsai, topiary, and espalier all share methods for shaping and training the growth of woody shrubs and trees. With a clear picture of the final result in mind, pick branches and foliage to keep or remove, bend, and fix in desired positions, or clip to a form. You'll need sharp bypass pruners, plastic plant tape, stiff wire rods, and your plants as you practice these techniques:

A To create stylized shapes on dwarf trees such as juniper, spruce, or maple, selectively remove some of the lateral limbs and foliage.

B Use chaff protection and looped ties to bend larger tree branches, reforming them. Use braces to bend them upward.

C Reshape branches by bending them in a sequence of small steps over several weeks or months, binding them with tape to stiff wire rods.

D Gradually train espaliered branches to a sturdy lattice frame by binding them with tape and selectively pruning.

E Create topiary by growing ivy or privet on a shaped wire mesh form, pinch-pruning runners and leaves as they form to keep them ½ in. (12 mm) from the form.

INDOOR SPRING BULBS

Do you eagerly anticipate the first flowers of spring? If you provide favorable conditions indoors, you can trick many bulbs into blooming during winter, well before they normally would flower outdoors. The technique is called forcing—stimulating a plant to bloom out of season.

Although many bulbs can be enticed to bloom in winter, amaryllis, hyacinth, and paperwhite narcissus are by far the easiest. Some other bulbs that respond well to forcing include some varieties of crocuses and tulips, Chinese sacred lily (*Narcissus tazetta*), 'Soleil d'Or' (another *N. Tazetta* cultivar), *Iris danfordiae*, and *I. reticulata*.

Two methods exist for forcing bulbs, and both are fairly simple—water forcing and soil forcing. Water forcing can be used to grow crocus, hyacinth, or narcissus. Add water to an hourglass-shaped container, then place the bulb just above the water. So-called hyacinth jars are made especially for this purpose. Keep the bulb itself dry; its roots soon will grow down and into the water, and the bulb will then send up shoots and flowers. Another method of water forcing is to closely plant the bulbs in a shallow pot of pebbles, sand, vermiculite, or perlite. These media don't provide nutrients but serve to hold the plant secure and upright [see Paperwhites in Water, this pg.].

(Below, right) Hyacinths are quick to flower after planting, provided that you allow them to develop roots and shoots before moving them into the light.

(Inset) White tulip surrounded with a circle of lily-of-the-valley makes a cheerful early-spring planting that seems to glow in a subdued-light setting.

PAPERWHITES IN WATER

Paperwhites are a delightful addition to the home with pert white flowers and a strong fragrance. Grow single paperwhites in a hyacinth forcing jar over water. For groups, plant bulbs in a shallow, drainless dish in sand or polished pebbles. Cover the bulbs with planting medium to their shoulders and water until moistened. Place them in a cool, dark location for 6 weeks. Water sparingly. Once their sprouts are 3–4 inches (75–100 mm) tall, move them to a dimly lit area for a week and then to an area with medium light for another week. After they've greened up, move them to their final destination in a bright area. Strong light helps stunt their growth, keeping the flower stalks compact and standing straight.

You also can grow every type of bulb in potting soil; some such as florist's amaryllis, or *Hippeastrum × hybridus*, require it [see Forcing Layered Bulbs in Soil, next pg.]. Once planted, place forced bulbs in a cool, dark area while they form a strong root structure, for 4–7 weeks. When they sprout 3–4 inches (75–100 mm) of green growth, remove the bulbs from the dark area to a dimly lit, warmer area for about a week, and then move them into a medium-lit area for another week or so. Once they have greened up, put them in their final location, a bright spot with indirect sun. Water them when the surface of the medium dries.

Buy bulbs when they become available in garden stores in autumn, and place them in a paper bag with punched holes or a plastic net bag. Prechill crocus, hyacinth, and tulips in a refrigerator's vegetable keeper for at least 6 weeks before planting. Keep them separate from foods, especially apples that release ethylene gas which causes bulbs to rot.

FORCING LAYERED BULBS IN SOIL

Forcing layered plantings of spring-blooming bulbs in soil gives you colorful blossoms throughout winter. Gather a paper sack, a large, deep container, two cultivars of bulbs that have different bloom seasons and planting depths, gloves, pea gravel, potting soil, a hand trowel, and a watering can, and follow these steps:

1 Fill a paper sack with slightly dampened sphagnum moss, nestle your bulbs in the moss, and place the sack into a refrigerator's vegetable keeper for 8–10 weeks before planting. Some bulbs come prechilled.

2 Remove the bulbs from the refrigerator. Prepare a pot by lining its bottom with pea gravel and filling it with 3 in. (75 mm) of potting soil. Compact the soil.

3 Plant the largest, deepest species in the first layer. Crowd the bulbs into the pot. Cover them to their neck with soil, gently pressing and compacting it.

Warning

Sphagnum moss may contain fungal spores that can cause allergic reactions in sensitive individuals. Avoid hazard by wearing latex gloves to handle sphagnum moss.

4 Plant a smaller species above the large bulbs in a layer, again crowding them into the pot. Fill the container with with soil to within 1 in. (25 mm) of the rim.

6 In a few weeks, the bulbs will sprout and bloom. Keep them 65–70°F (18–21°C) during the day and 60–65°F (16–18°C) at night for flowers that will last 2–3 weeks in most cultivars.

5 Thoroughly water the pot, and place it in a protected spot outdoors or in an unheated, indoor location where it will be safe from freezing temperatures.

Make theme
and color the
key to arranging
your plants
and creating
pleasing effects
that everyone
will enjoy

Arrangement and Placement

Have you ever walked into a home filled with houseplants and instantly felt peaceful and serene? Has a clustering of colorful flowering plants on a coffee table left you mesmerized? You easily can duplicate these wonderful effects with plants in your own home. Positioned properly, houseplants can make your indoors so stunning and welcoming that you will feel as if you're on vacation in your own home. A few simple guidelines will help you achieve the look and feel you want.

You might wonder where to start. One good place is in the media. The pages of current periodicals and home decorating programs on television are full of ideas, hints, tips, and insights that will help guide you as you begin decorating your home with greenery and flowering plants. With your ideas in mind, you will next want to choose the effect that you wish to create. From that decision eventually will come both your theme and color palette to accompany the plant choices that you make for your rooms.

In the following pages, you will uncover the secrets of creating a dazzling interior, using plants to highlight just about any aspect of your decor. You will learn how to match plants to your home's design theme, whether it's contemporary, traditional, formal, period, southwestern, or cottage cozy. You will become a master at integrating the intricate details of your decor with houseplants, matching fabrics and wall coverings to plants, and creating effects with their varied leaf textures, sizes, shapes, and colors. You also will see how you can use a color wheel to mix complementary or contrasting bloom and foliage colors in the same planting. And finally, you'll discover ideas for presenting friends and loved ones with the ultimate houseplant gifts, including step-by-step instructions for creating a gift plant.

Arranging and placing houseplants is a task that you'll do frequently. Each time a piece of furniture or a window covering is changed or a new item is added to your home, you'll find yourself balancing your houseplants, too. If you follow the pointers in this chapter, your houseplants will be more than accessories to your furnishings; they'll be integral to your home's decor.

These plants seem a natural part of this family game room. Their placement at the hearth accentuates the strong vertical lines of the fireplace and provides balance to the linear shape of the pool table.

PLANTS AND THEME

Remember how you carefully matched your wallpaper to your window coverings and ended up with a well-designed room? Do the same with plants. With a little imagination, you can create delightful themes using plants, fabrics, and wall coverings.

The design possibilities in matching or contrasting colors are nearly endless. You can highlight purple floral wallpaper with purple African violets set in an ivory-colored antique dish. Put a basket of pink polka-dot plant in a bathroom with hot pink painted walls, then add bright pink and green towels for even more color intensity. In a solarium with butter yellow walls and green garden furniture, choices abound for matching foliage and bloom colors to your decor. Emphasize plants with graceful foliage such as *Ficus benjamina*, asparagus fern, maidenhair fern, rabbit's-foot fern, and large palms. Offset the yellow walls with flowering plants in bright colors such as anthurium, goldfish plant, and lipstick plant. Or bring out the yellow tones by introducing a light green and cream arrangement by using arrowhead vine, variegated green and yellow ivy, and a white or yellow orchid, creating a soft palette that will blend the colors together.

You can achieve dazzling results by echoing botanical prints or wallpaper. Match a grape ivy lattice–motif wallpaper border with an actual hanging basket overflowing with grape ivy. Offset an herb-themed wallpaper or framed botanical print in your kitchen with a windowsill herb garden.

Emphasize a theme for more plant options. Play the bold green leaves and orange and blue flowers of bird-of-paradise off a jungle-print wallpaper in a child's room; plant it in a rattan pot for added effect. In a room that has organic features such as wicker furniture, rattan-patterned wallpaper, and bamboo flooring, add a mature corn plant with its brown, leathery single stem and graceful variegated foliage. A study with Danish modern teak furniture takes on a vibrant look when highlighted by forced bulbs in glass containers full of rocks. Good choices for forcing include tulips, crocus, and hyacinth. In a southwestern-themed room, set up a cactus and succulent table near a bright window. Include a wide range of foliage shades such as deep green, yellow, medium green, and lime green. And remember to add visual interest by varying shapes. Try long pointy-leaved succulents and a gray and hairy old-man cactus.

You also can use plants to create transitions; for instance, to separate a light airy living room from a dark hallway, use a row of palms. Make the transition from hallway to living room complete by adding a variegated foliage plant such as a pink and green caladium in the center of the coffee table. In need of a frame to create interest for a ho-hum window? Create a foliage border out of pothos or trailing philodendron that you can look through to the outdoors.

Plant matching in three forms: coordination with a wallpaper border (top); color harmony of a plant, its container, and a vase (middle); and integration of forms between the architectural elements and the plant's foliage. Use these ideas in your home.

CREATING FORMAL ARRANGEMENTS

T he best houseplant arrangements are those with a central theme. Plants may have varied heights, foliage forms, or bloom colors yet work together because they complete a tropical motif, blend leaf colors attractively, or have a sculptural quality. Arrange houseplants in groups, starting with coordinated containers and a plant stand that features varied levels. Choose one or more of these popular options for the various rooms of your home:

A Green and variegated foliage with a variety of leaf patterns makes lush arrangements suited to bright, solarium-like settings and wicker furniture.

B Massed color from a single species such as African violet or tuberous begonia coordinates bloom colors for ever-changing appeal.

C Mixed heights provide vertical relief, filling the field at eye level while showcasing your dramatic or unusual plants.

D Placing those plants with bold horizontal forms alongside those with equally strong vertical shapes adds drama to fill a square or rectangular space or corner.

E Pairing hanging plants with others on stands fills a wall with color, texture, shadows, and visual interest.

F Dividing a space with plants, making a living wall, or creating an organic greenery nook offers an alternative to ornate furnishings and strong-patterned upholstery.

INTEGRATING WITH COLOR

The wide variety of colors in houseplant foliage and blooms makes it possible to decorate any room in your home. As a matter of fact, going to your nursery or garden center and seeing the broad array of available flowers and foliage—much of it variegated—is similar to browsing through wallcovering and upholstery samples. Your choices are almost limitless.

Flowering plants are an obvious choice when it comes to decorating with color. Choose pink anthuriums to pick up the coral in a bedspread, for instance, or offset the vivid red of a begonia with the scarlet in the living room draperies. A grouping of pastel-colored cyclamen can make the muted pink and purple flowers in a bathroom wallpaper come alive.

Plants with variegated leaves offer an even larger realm from which to choose, mix, and match. Coleus have attractive velvetlike patterns of green, silver, white, and yellow that can mimic the pattern in a sofa. Purple velvet plant easily can offset the rich red-wine tones of living room wallpaper. Peacock plant, *Calathea makoyana*, with its dark green, lime, and red leaves looks especially stunning when placed in the center of a maroon tablecloth. And polka-dot plant adds a charming touch to a young child's pink and white bedroom. These are but a few of the many ways you can use colorful foliage to spruce up your decor.

From the realm of green foliage plants, comes a wide variety from which you can choose. Let the dark green, glossy leaves of *Dracaena* 'Janet Craig' play off wooden furniture and light green curtains. Or create a grouping of plants in shades of cream, green, and white, and highlight them against an off-white wall. Lime green plants such as arrowhead vine, dieffenbachia, and ivy combine well for such an arrangement.

Be sure to consider lighting when you choose plant colors for your decor. A room with bright lighting may wash out the strong primary colors displayed in a tulip arrangement, while that same grouping can become luminous in a more subdued setting. Incorporate whites and silvers for darker areas; they seem to glow in dim light. Most flowering plants prefer sunny areas, but the peace lily with its ivory flowers often will bloom in dim light. Or, if you really want to create a stunning focal point, spotlight a specimen plant such as a white orchid under a single plant light.

The precise shade and hue of colors in your home sometimes can be a challenge to recall in the nursery or garden center. A visual aid is helpful; gather paint chip samples and paste them onto a card to help you remember the color combinations and make comparisons easy.

USING A COLOR WHEEL

1 Consult the color wheel as you choose a primary flower color. Here, red roses were picked as the first color choice, a starting hue that will contrast naturally with its own deep green foliage.

Color wheels, readily available at hobby and art stores, are used by artists and designers to visualize the hues they will use for paintings and other projects. Indoor gardeners can benefit from using a color wheel to plan their pots—especially mixed plantings. The wheel presents the primary colors—red, yellow, and blue—interspersed with their complements—orange, green, and violet. Some wheels also are divided into "cool" and "warm" palettes. Use your wheel to create mixed plantings, following these easy steps:

2 Pick the second color from among the hues found to either side of your primary choice. Here, red violet blooms of a pansy orchid were picked as the adjacent color.

3 Finally, choose blooms of a color that is complementary to your primary or adjacent color selection. Here, yellow roses will contrast with the orchid's red violet blooms.

5 The completed arrangement features two roses in red and yellow, accompanied by the pansy orchid in a second pot—orchids need bark rather than soil for their roots.

4 Choose a pot finished with a neutral color and with space to accommodate the mature height and spread of the plants. Crowd the plants tightly into the container for best results.

SHARING HOUSEPLANT GIFTS

Few gifts are as long-lasting or memorable as houseplants. What better way to brighten the home of a friend or family member than to give a piece of living greenery that can be enjoyed for months or even years to come?

Carefully choose your houseplant gifts. Before giving a plant as a present, consider the recipient's decorating tastes and the growing conditions of the plant's new home. Does it have a formal, more modern decor where a single orchid could create a striking focal point? Or is the home more eclectic and informal, calling for a cheery basket of mixed foliage plants? Is there a bright room where flowering houseplants will thrive? Or would it be safer to choose plants with variegated or green foliage? If the lighting is especially dim, choose from the many low-light houseplants. Cast-iron plant, Chinese evergreen, dieffenbachia, peperomia, prayer plant, and sansevieria are all low-light plants that make pleasing gifts. There are even flowering plants that do well in low light such as anthurium and orange jasmine, or *Murraya paniculata*. This latter plant flowers most of the year and has a heavenly orange-blossom scent that's sure to delight its recipient.

In general, it's best to choose plants on the small side when you're planning a gift. A large floor plant or vining hanging basket also might be welcome, but it's best to check with the recipient first. Choose plants that can easily fit into most spaces with very little rearranging, and keep the decor in mind when you select a container.

To give your houseplant gift a festive look, adorn it with ribbons, balloons, or accessories such as colorful ceramic plant markers. And for an extra-special touch, create your own custom plant-care tag with the detailed instructions for the specific watering, fertilizing, and care needs of your gift plant. You even can include a small bottle of appropriate houseplant food or a watering can. Then just add a gift card and your houseplant will be all ready to go calling on its new owner.

(Right) Give your plant gift a watering the evening before you plan to present it to its recipient. A loose paper gift bag is the best wrapping, since it allows both air and light to reach the plant.

(Bottom) Choose a decorative pot or basket that matches the furnishings and wallcoverings of the plant's new home.

CREATING A GIFT WITH PLANTS

Sharing houseplants with friends adds another dimension of pleasure to your gardening hobby. Many perennial houseplants naturally divide or can be propagated to yield offspring [see Propagating New Plants, pg. 76]. A green gift comprises the plants, an attractive container, and some finishing touches such as clear cellophane wrap and a bow. Gather these items, your potting soil, and hand tools, then follow these steps:

1 When plants propagated from your houseplants have reached mature size, they are ready to become gifts.

2 Choose a container with the particular recipient in mind. Use clues taken from hobbies, collectibles, or home decor to match container and plants.

3 If you're using a variety of plants, place tall species at the center and trailing varieties along the edges. Water the planting thoroughly, then allow it to drain.

4 Use breathable cellophane to wrap the gift, adding air holes every 4 in. (10 cm). Avoid using polypropylene wrap. A staple at the peak will hold the wrap in place.

5 Add a decorative ribbon and bow for a finishing touch. A ceramic figurine also can be included for accent color.

If you care for your houseplants properly and provide consistent maintenance, they will brighten your home with lush foliage for many years, becoming an integral part of your home's decor.

In the following pages, you will learn how to keep your plants healthy, beginning with proper watering. When you water your plants correctly, at the right interval, in the right manner, and with the right amount, you will be rewarded with plants that respond with vigorous growth. Surprisingly, there's more than one method of irrigation, and some plants should receive one over another. Here you'll find pointers to avoid under- and overwatering as well as step-by-step instructions for deep watering your houseplants. You'll also learn about your plants' nutritional needs. Feeding plants the right fertilizer at the proper time in the correct amount is an important skill to master. You'll see how to select fertilizers and the best ways to apply them.

In this chapter, you'll find information about trellises and plant supports as well as how to use them to show off your houseplants to their best advantage. To keep your plants vigorous and shapely, you'll find detailed directions on how to prune and pinch them, controlling their growth. So that you can spread your plants around and give them to friends and family, you'll get detailed instructions on several techniques for propagating new plants from existing ones. Following step-by-step, illustrated demonstrations, you'll try techniques from stem cuttings to root division, and you'll learn which method to use for which plants. You'll also find out when and how to repot crowded plants so they remain healthy and vigorous. Finally, you'll learn the secrets to spotting and controlling pests and diseases with an easy-to-use chart.

Indoor gardening means caring for your plants on almost a daily routine. You'll need to check the dampness of soil here, pinch a wayward shoot there, glance at the underside of a leaf, prune away a withered branch. Most of us find these activities fun and relaxing. With the proper care you'll give your plants, your indoor garden will match the one in your dreams.

Learn the secrets of watering, feeding, staking, pruning, and growing new plants, as you prevent pests and diseases

Houseplant Care

Caring for many houseplants is easiest when you have the right tools and they're kept close at hand. Some of the best tools are those made especially for indoor gardening. They are small in size and fit the needs of houseplants better than garden tools.

WATERING HOUSEPLANTS

Watering is the most important aspect of plant care. Although it might seem a good idea to put your plants on a watering schedule, it's best for them that you water only when they actually need it. This will vary from plant to plant and season to season. Surprisingly, the symptoms of both under- and overwatering include browning leaf tips and a wilted appearance. Always use chlorine- and chloramine-free water to water your plants, and avoid using any water from a water-softening or hard-water treatment system. Collected rain water is ideal.

A variety of techniques exist for checking to see if your plants need watering. The "finger test" is practically infallible. Stick your finger into the soil up to the first finger joint. Damp soil means caution—you should wait to water most plants. Or try a moisture meter—a pronged instrument that is stuck into the soil and indicates the amount of moisture present. Another method is the "pick-up" test. Light weight can be an indication that a plant needs watering. Oftentimes a plant will "flag" before wilting—the leaves appear slightly limp and lose their sheen. If this is the case, check to see that it needs watering, as flagging and wilting also are symptoms of overwatering [see Under- and Overwatering, below].

Helpful watering aids include a slow-release water reservoir, water-retaining polymer to mix with your plant soil, an electronic moisture meter with a long probe to measure how damp the soil is deep in the rootball, a mister for foliage and flowers, and a sturdy watering can equipped with a long extension nozzle to reach deep into the center of plants.

The way you water a plant also is important. Most plants do best when water is applied deep within the soil. It's best to dunk your plants in a sink or bucket filled with water. Always use tepid water—cold water has been known to cause root damage and leaf spotting—and leave the plant in the water until all bubbling ceases. You'll probably have to leave large plants in place and water from above. Irrigate until excess water flows out of the bottom of the pot and collects in the cachepot, as this ensures that the entire rootball has been moistened. Thorough watering, regardless of method, leaches salts from the soil. After a half-hour, check for standing water in the saucer or cachepot and remove any excess with a turkey baster; leaving plants sitting in water can promote fungal disease [see Indoor Plant Diseases, pg. 84].

Some plants—fuzzy-leaved varieties such as African violet and the pickaback plant—should be watered from below, or via a wick system. Water splashed onto leaves of these plants will mar them and quickly leads to rot. Watering from below is a good procedure for any plant that is susceptible to crown rot.

To water from below, fill a saucer or other drainless pot with tepid water and place the plant inside. Water will be drawn by osmosis—wicking—into the dry soil. Cachepots are perfect for this purpose. After watering, remember to empty the outer pot so that the bottom of the growing container avoids contact with standing water.

Should a lapse in watering occur, take immediate steps to deep water your plant, especially if the soil has dried out substantially. Submerge the plant in tepid water and give it a good soaking.

UNDER- AND OVERWATERING

It's easy to master the art of proper watering if you keep a few tips in mind.

Test each plant's soil before watering—for best results, use more than one method. For instance, you might use both a moisture meter and feel the soil with your finger; if still unsure, pick up the pot to see if it seems lightweight. Remember to balance the needs of plants that require constant moisture with those best watered after their soil dries.

Rather than watering on a schedule, frequently check your plants' soil. Regular examinations will assure that you remember each plant and its watering requirements. Consider approximately how often your plants require watering and make sure to check them around the same time every few days. Water them deeply, allow them to drain, and remove any standing water from their cachepots or saucers.

Self-watering pots can extend considerably the time between waterings. Remember, though, that these pots should be used only for plants that require constant, even moisture.

DEEP WATERING HOUSEPLANTS

Proper watering—frequency and quantity—is important to any houseplant's health. Remember that only a few plants thrive in evenly moist conditions; most should be watered, then their soil should be allowed to dry before another watering takes place. Regular waterings should occur each time a plant's soil dries. At least once a month, deep water your plants to remove mineral salts, following these easy steps:

1 Whenever soil shows signs of mineral deposits, or about once a month, move your houseplants to a deep sink or outdoor basin in a shady spot that is sheltered from wind.

2 Fill the sink or basin with tepid water up to the rim of the plant's container or just slightly above it.

3 Allow the plant to remain submerged in the water about 5 minutes after all of the air bubbles have been released.

4 Remove the plant from the water and allow it to completely drain. If visible salt deposits remain, repeat the process a second time.

5 When the plant has drained, apply foliar fertilizer to the plant's leaves at half the package-recommended strength.

FEEDING AND FERTILIZING

Although plants make their own food from sunlight, air, and nutrients, they require dissolved minerals to start this complex chemical process. It's generally a good idea to supply some extra plant food in the form of fertilizers. Signs that your houseplants could use a feeding include yellowing leaves, less new growth, smaller new growth when you get it, and failure to bloom.

Plants need at least three macronutrients to survive: nitrogen (N), which helps create new growth and leads to the production of chlorophyll; phosphorus (P), which enables a plant to have healthy roots and buds and allows a plant's fruit and seeds to ripen; and potassium (K), which plays an important role in photosynthesis and water management and strengthens plants against pests and disease. The N–P–K ratio by weight is shown numerically— 5–10–10, for instance—on fertilizer packages. The best houseplant food also contains important micro- and trace nutrients, which are essential to complete plant health.

Houseplants generally need the most fertilizing in spring and summer when they are likely to be growing rapidly. The needs of houseplants vary widely, however—some may require monthly, quarterly, or annual feedings, while others should receive a dilute solution of liquid fertilizer with every watering. Whatever the recommended timing, it's important to avoid overfertilizing. Too much fertilizer can lead to leaf-tip burn and fallen brown leaves—also warning signs of too-low humidity. Even if you feed properly, however, most fertilizers accumulate in the soil over time. It's a good idea to water deeply to leach fertilizer from your plants' soil every month or so [see Deep Watering Houseplants, pg. 69].

Feeding correctly is important to houseplant health. Buy a fertilizer designed for houseplants. These come in many forms—liquids, spikes, powders, tablets, granules, and foliar sprays. Liquid fertilizers are easy to apply and spread more evenly. For extra-quick results, try foliar feeding—spraying fertilizer directly on the leaves; make sure that the fertilizer is specifically formulated for such use. A wide variety of synthetic fertilizers exist on the market, or you can try an organic food such as worm castings, bat and bird guano, fish emulsion, or sea kelp.

Many factors affect the uptake of nutrients into plants, including the pH of the soil and water—the degree of its acidity or alkalinity. Many houseplants do best in acidic conditions. If its soil becomes very alkaline, your plant may develop mineral deficiency conditions such as chlorosis—an inability to take up iron—causing new leaves to be stunted and yellow. If you see such symptoms after fertilizing, test the soil pH with a test kit or meter and adjust your care as the instrument or kit instructions recommend.

NUTRITIONAL NEEDS

Most houseplants do well with a general all-purpose fertilizer and regular potting soil. Some, however, have specific nutritional needs. For this reason, it's important to carefully review the nutrient requirements of each of your plants. Orchids, for example, must have their bark replaced every year or decomposition can rot the roots, which then fail to take up nutrients. Other plants—citrus, for instance—require an especially acidic environment or they become chlorotic and will fail to bloom and produce fruit. Acidify the soil with sulfur, conifer leaf mold, or another acidic compost.

(Above) Fertilizer stakes have slow-release nutrients contained in a neutral, dissolvable base. Because they feed houseplants continually, they are best used for plants that have continual growth rather than dormant periods when they rest.

(Below) Read completely and follow the package instructions exactly when mixing plant food for your houseplants. Too much nitrogen can burn their foliage, and too weak a mixture can cause them to lose vigor.

APPLYING FERTILIZER

B ecause houseplants are planted in containers with little soil, fertilizing is a necessary part of their care. It's best to feed your plants on a regular schedule, tailoring the fertilizer to the plant. Some species require acidic fertilizers, while most do not [see Encyclopedia of Common Houseplants, pg. 87]. Choose either method shown, following these steps:

Applying Granular Fertilizer

1 Always thoroughly water your houseplant the day before applying granular fertilizer.

2 Carefully measure the fertilizer, and follow exactly the package recommendations, spreading it evenly on the soil surface.

3 Using a small hand fork, work the fertilizer into the soil. Apply water and allow the container to drain.

Applying Foliar Fertilizer

1 Mix the foliar fertilizer concentrate or powder with water, diluting it as recommended on the package. Fill a hand applicator bottle.

2 Spray a mist of dilute foliar fertilizer solution onto the plant's foliage and stem until they are thoroughly wet.

3 Water the plant after applying fertilizer, allowing the soil to drain. The foliage should be dry before it is exposed to direct sunlight.

TRELLISES AND SUPPORTS

In their native environments, many plants have trees and other woody plants on which to grow. Mimic nature by giving your houseplants a structure to cling to, and often they'll thrive. You can find plant supports and trellises in a wide variety of styles and sizes.

Those plants that benefit from some type of support fall into three categories. First, there are plants with a lax stem or large flower head that require staking to keep the plant upright for best display. For these use an unobtrusive green or black stake. Gently insert it into the soil near the plant stem and attach it to the plant with stretchy green plastic garden tape, which expands as the plant grows.

Second is a large category of rambling, trailing, and climbing plants. Use a trellis for these plants and direct them to grow wherever you desire, including up a wall or across a room. Most need some help winding onto the trellis support, so attach them with plastic garden tape. Vines in this group include arrowhead vine, hoya, pothos, and wandering Jew. There are a few—some ivy such as *Cissus antartica*, for example—that will anchor themselves to the trellis with tough fibrous holdfasts.

The third category includes plants with aerial roots that prefer a continuously moist, moss-covered pole on which to fasten and climb. The Swiss-cheese plant and philodendrons are in this group. These plants should be wound around and attached loosely to the poles, which can be found ready-made at nurseries or garden centers. You also can make your own; wearing gloves, fill a wire cage with sphagnum moss [see Installing Plant Stakes, next pg.].

A wide variety of stakes and supports are available in bamboo, metal, plastic, rattan, wire, and wood. When selecting a trellis, consider the size of your existing plant and its pot. Supports made of metal will be heavier; make sure that the container can bear the weight without toppling. If necessary, put the pot inside a heavier container to add more support.

It's best to install trellises and supports at the time of planting, as later installation can cause root damage. Of course, it's sometimes necessary to place supports in existing plants. Do so with care, determining in advance exactly where the support is needed to avoid multiple tries. Set the support as deep as possible and wind the plant around its base immediately to add stability. If more support is needed, wire the support to the container or plant stand.

For best results, keep a few things in mind when staking and securing plants to trellises. Tie the plant to the support in several locations, so that it isn't vulnerable to breaking at just one tie point. Use stretchy plastic tie tape to prevent girdling the plants' stems, and resecure or replace when necessary.

(Right) Choose from the wide variety of plant supports and trellises that are available.

(Below) The arrowhead plant in in this basket will soon reach the top of its supporting post and need repotting into a container with a new, taller, sphagnum moss pole.

INSTALLING PLANT STAKES

1 Use wire cutters, wire ties, and needle-nosed pliers to make a hardware cloth column, 2–3 in. (50–75 mm) in diameter.

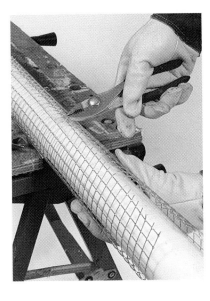

Large trailing or vining plants look best when supported on fibrous or sphagnum moss–filled stakes. In nature, many tropical plants climb trees to heights of 40 ft. (12 m) or more. Make a stake by filling a narrow column of hardware cloth with moss, or obtain a fibrous stake at your nursery or garden center, then support your plants by following these easy steps:

2 Fill the center of the wire stake with dry sphagnum moss. The moss will hold the moisture and slowly release humidity to the plant's foliage.

3 Make three vertical cuts in the base of the stake, each 3 in. (75 mm) long. Fold out each wire flap to make a support.

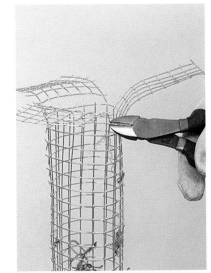

4 Protect the pot's drain hole with wire mesh. Mount the stake in the container, covering the hardware cloth flange with pea gravel to stabilize it.

5 Plant your houseplant in the container and fill with soil. Water thoroughly, and allow the pot to drain. As the plant grows, train it up the stake using stretchy plant tape.

PRUNING AND PINCHING

Few houseplants need regular pruning, though many require some form of pinching back to keep them shapely. For the few that do need pruning to maintain their vigor and appearance, clipping and cutting once a season will keep them compact, dense, and healthy. In some cases, pruning also is necessary to remove dead or damaged wood.

Vining plants such as pothos produce trailing stems that can become lanky and leggy, with long gaps between leaves. When you shorten such stems by pinching off the growing tips, you encourage the plant to put out new, bushier growth, and the new leaves will grow closer together. Always pinch just above a leaf node—where there already is a leaf—or at a bump in the stem where a leaf stalk formerly was attached. New growth will come from that nascent bud. Pinching close to the bud is important because any extra bare stem will die back and could become diseased. Generally, your thumb and forefinger make good pinchers because most new growth is tender. If not, use pruners or a sharp knife. Avoid leaving any jagged edges, which also can harbor disease.

Some plants require regular pinching, while others need it only once or twice a year. Use care when pinching plants that flower to avoid cutting off young buds. Get to know each plant's flowering cycle before doing any pinching. Plants that do best with regular pinching include arrowhead plant—assuming you want it to be bushy—coleus, grape ivy, Swedish ivy, vining philodendron, polka-dot plant, pothos, and wandering Jew. Plants grown within a definite framework—espaliered plants, bonsai, and topiary—also need frequent pinch training.

Houseplants that require occasional pruning for shaping and removal of dead or crossing stems and branches in spring include *Ficus benjamina*, fittonia, and pilea. Lipstick plant, which should be pruned back to about a third after flowering, is one of many flowering plants that require seasonal pinching or pruning. To encourage reflowering in columnea, cut back older branches by a third to a half in spring.

Many plants require very little, if any, pruning, but grooming these plants by removing old leaves is still a good idea, as it makes the plants look nicer overall. To encourage even growth, rotate your plants a quarter turn every week. This will cause them to adjust to the room's source of light and make them grow evenly.

Deadheading spent flowers on an azalea is done mostly for cosmetic enhancement as its blooms fade. On other plants, removing spent flowers will cause new buds to develop and extend its flowering.

PRUNING HOUSEPLANTS

Some broad-leaved houseplants become leggy when they grow in areas with limited light; others may require pruning to direct their growth or make them more compact. In either case, use a hand bypass pruner to trim them, following these steps:

1 Remove and destroy any dead, diseased, or infected branches or foliage, cutting them off parallel to and flush with the main stem or lateral branch.

2 Shape the outer perimeter of the foliage by cutting off any shoots that extend beyond the imaginary line that defines the houseplant's silhouette.

3 Remove about a quarter of the interior lateral branches of the plant, opening its center to the light. Choose those branches that cross through the plant's center.

5 For an arching or weeping appearance, remove upward-growing shoots, leaving those that recurve toward the soil.

4 To create an upright, treelike appearance, cut away lower limbs along the main stem and any suckers that grow from the root crown.

PROPAGATING NEW PLANTS

Gardeners easily can duplicate most of their favorite plants without setting foot in a nursery or garden center. Starting new plants from old ones—propagating—is a fun and rewarding way to develop healthy plants from aging specimens and to replace hard-to-find favorites. Most houseplants can be propagated at home, a task best accomplished during spring and summer.

The method most often used to propagate houseplants is to take cuttings. A cutting is taken from a parent plant and encouraged to form its own roots. There are two types of cuttings—stem cuttings and leaf cuttings. To produce a stem cutting, snip from the plant a healthy young shoot that has at least two or three leaf nodes—points at which leaves attach to the stem. Insert the cut shoot into a rooting medium such as water, perlite, or vermiculite. In a month or so, it will form roots, creating a new plant genetically identical to its parent. Leaf cuttings are done in a similar manner, using a leaf instead of a stem. Stem cuttings are better for some types of plants; leaf cuttings are best for others. Apply rooting hormone to increase success when taking cuttings.

Another way to propagate plants is through root division—separating plants at the root zone so you end up with two or more plants. This is usually done when a plant has outgrown its pot. Propagate African violet, cast-iron plant, asparagus fern, Boston fern, peace lily, sansevieria, spider plant, and zebra plant in this manner during periods when their growth slows or they become dormant.

Newly transplanted or rooted plants require ideal growing conditions for the first 6–8 weeks of their life. Rear them under glass or beneath a full-spectrum grow light that gives them both heat and brightness.

AIR LAYERING

If a single-stemmed plant has become tall and lanky, air layering is the best method for propagation. This technique enables you to get a large plant from a single cutting and also is a productive way to prune.

At the point where you'd like to shorten the plant, cut a notch halfway through the stem just below a leaf node. Hold the cut open with a toothpick and apply rooting hormone powder, available at garden centers, to the inside of the cut. Wearing gloves, wrap the wound with moistened sphagnum moss and seal it with plastic wrap. Keep the moss moist by periodically misting. In a month or so, the moss should fill with roots. When this occurs, cut the parent stem at a spot just below the new plant's roots and repot it. The mother plant should branch from where you made the cut.

For some plants, layering works well. This technique encourages a new plant to form roots while still attached to the parent. Pickaback plant and spider plant make the process easy by providing ready-to-root plantlets. Other plants—fittonia, ivy, and pothos—lack this helpful trait but are just as easy to root. Bring plantlets or plant tips into contact with the soil, pin them down, and keep them moist; they quickly will produce new roots that can be cut from the mother plant. You can either layer in separate pots or pin plant tips in the same container. Certain woody-stemmed plants must be air-layered instead [see Air Layering, above].

Some houseplants also can be grown from seed.

REPRODUCTION WITH STEM CUTTINGS

1 Choose a new sprout, cutting it cleanly at a slight angle with a razor blade or knife. Carefully strip the cutting of all foliage leaves and buds except the topmost leaf.

Many succulent houseplants and some with woody stems can be propagated easily by rooting foliage cuttings. Plants that result are identical to their parent; note that some patented plants are subject to restrictions that bar vegetative reproduction. New foliage spikes are best for rooting. Gather your plant; a clean, sharp, thin-bladed knife or single-edged razor blade; a pot filled with sterile potting soil; support stakes; a clear plastic bag; and rooting hormone compound—available at garden stores or at nurseries—and follow these steps:

2 Dip each cutting into rooting hormone powder to stimulate the nascent growth buds on their cut stems to sprout roots.

3 Set the cutting deeply into the pot's wet potting soil. About a third of the stem should show above the soil.

4 Set three stakes in the pot's edges. Place the pot into the plastic bag and loosely tie it to the container.

6 Set the pot in a warm, brightly lit spot with indirect sunlight. In 2–4 weeks, the cutting will have sprouted roots and should be transplanted.

5 Using a blade, slit four to six airholes in the plastic, each about ½ in. (12 mm) long.

ROOT DIVISION

D ivide houseplants that grow in clusters, those with fans of foliage, and those that have low tufts of leaves after they bloom, or whenever they become crowded. Gather a hand trowel, two hand forks, a garden spade, leather gloves, and a sharp knife, then follow these easy steps:

1 Use the knife to free the edges of the rootball from the pot. Carefully invert the container, supporting the rootball with your open palm.

2 Gently slide the plant's container from the rootball while avoiding tugging on the plant, its foliage, or its stem. Divide the plant by choosing one of the options below.

3 Replant the divisions, each in its own container. Water with liquid fertilizer diluted to half the package-recommended rate, settling the soil.

Option
A For fibrous-rooted plants, use two hand forks to pry the individual plant clusters apart, making separate sections that each contain a complete root, crown, and leaves.

Option
B For rhizomatous plants, use a sharp knife to divide each rhizome into V-shaped pieces, each with at least two growth points.

Option
C For large plants with thick, heavy roots, use a trowel or spade to cut down between complete plant sections.

ROOTING NEW PLANTS

S ome houseplants reproduce themselves by runners or offsets— small plants that form on extended stems or their foliage tips. These infant plants can be cut from the parent and rooted to start a new houseplant. Gather your plant; a clean, sharp, thin-bladed shears or single-edged razor blade; and a pot filled with sterile potting soil, and follow these steps:

Rooting Runners

1 Encourage plants to form new runners by staking long foliage stems to the soil and keeping them moist. Keep the leaves from ground contact.

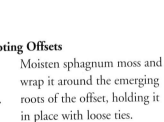

2 When the stem roots, cut it from the main plant using the sharp shears or razor blade. Allow it to grow independently for 2–3 weeks.

3 Transplant the young plant to its own container, watering and fertilizing it.

2 In 5–10 days, the offset will form roots. Cut the offset from the parent plant, and plant it in moist, sterile potting soil.

Rooting Offsets

1 Moisten sphagnum moss and wrap it around the emerging roots of the offset, holding it in place with loose ties.

3 Water every other day, keeping the soil evenly moist until the roots mature and the offset begins to grow new foliage.

REPOTTING CROWDED PLANTS

Although houseplants seldom need repotting, they eventually will become root-bound and require a new home. Roots emerging from the bottom of the pot, sluggish growth, and water rushing through the soil when it's watered are all signs that a plant needs repotting. Some plants actually crack their pots when their roots become tightly wound in a container. To check whether a plant needs repotting, remove it from its container and inspect its roots. It's time to repot if the plant's many tangled roots have nearly filled the rootball's soil; wait to repot if you mostly see potting soil.

At least 2 hours before repotting, water the plant well. It's sometimes necessary to free the plant from its existing pot by holding the plant's stem and soil surface steadily with one hand, inverting the pot with the other, and tapping the pot rim against a hard surface until it slides out. If the plant still refuses to budge, try running a sharp knife around the edge of the soil and then turning it over. In exceptional cases, you may have to break or cut the pot.

Choose a new container that's no more than 2 inches (50 mm) wider than the original, keeping the soil planting level the same. While it might seem a good idea to give a plant growing room with an even larger pot, excess soil around the plant roots will become waterlogged and can promote fungal disease infections.

After planting, water the plant well with a watering can or by soaking the entire pot in water. Drain the pot, then avoid watering again until the first inch (25 mm) or so of potting soil has dried out. Overwatering after repotting can cause the plant roots to develop fungal disease. If the soil is still wet, and the plant shows signs of wilting, mist it with water. Your plant may take some time to need a drink; most plants use less water when they are newly transplanted.

If you will be moving your plant to a different location, give it a few days to adjust to the new pot before placing it in its new home. When moving the plant, avoid transplant shock by finding a space with conditions similar to its prior home. Wait at least a month before fertilizing repotted plants again after planting. The best time to feed is when they begin to show a fair amount of new growth. This means a plant has successfully re-established itself and needs nutrients for continued growth.

Although houseplant owners often choose to repot a plant so that it can grow larger, it also is possible to repot a plant and keep it the same size. If you wish to maintain your plant's size, take it out of its container, slice off an inch (25 mm) of roots all around the rootball and set the plant into new soil. Because you have pruned its roots, you should strip away between a quarter and a third of its leaves, leaving the growth tips at the end of stems intact. As the plant develops new roots, its foliage will grow.

The yucca shown here had been growing in the same pot for 3 years and was beginning to lose vigor. It was repotted to prune its roots and replace about a third of the surrounding soil, which had become compacted.

REPLANTING TO LARGER CONTAINERS

Repotting—actually transplanting mature houseplants—becomes necessary whenever they become rootbound in their containers. The purpose of repotting is to unwind or cut encircling roots and provide new, loose soil. You'll also use the instructions given for new plantings [see Planting in Containers, pg. 47]. Gather your rootbound plant, a flat-bladed knife, a new container 2 in. (50 mm) wider than the old, pea gravel or filter fabric, and a hand trowel, then follow these easy steps:

1 Carefully free the plant from the container by sliding a knife vertically around its rim. Note the soil level on the plant.

2 Lay the container on its side and grasp the rootball. If necessary, cut the side of the container to loosen it from the soil. Slide the plant out.

3 Wash the rootball's sides with water, freeing soil and loosening roots. Unwind encircling roots.

4 Prune excess root growth, reducing about a third of the total by removing laterals from main root branches. Roots are delicate; use care when handling them.

5 Plant the houseplant into its new container, backfilling with soil to the same level on the plant as its original height.

6 Mix liquid fertilizer such as 5–10–10 at a quarter the label-recommended rate. Saturate the rootball with fertilizer solution. If root pruning was extensive, strip an equivalent amount of foliage to help the plant balance its nutritional needs until it has adjusted.

CONTROLLING HOUSEPLANT PESTS

Even the best indoor gardens sometimes experience an infestation of aphids or an outbreak of mealybugs. Pests are a natural part of gardening, indoors and out. What you do when you first find a pest has great impact on whether your plant will overcome the infestation. Regular inspections are critical, because they allow you to detect a problem before it spreads.

The key to controlling houseplant pests is recognizing the signs and symptoms of various pests and then quickly acting. Several common pests may appear; each has its own telltale signs.

Aphids are small, fleshy insects that come in many colors—black, brown, green, red, and yellow. They generally cluster and feed on new plant growth, sucking sap out of leaves, causing holes, and distorting new growth. They excrete a sticky honeydew liquid, which can drop on furniture. Spraying the plant with water daily for a period of several days greatly reduces aphid populations.

Mealybugs are white, cottony pests that suck sap from plant leaves and produce a sticky residue. They thrive in tight areas on plants such as the joints where leaves attach to the stem. If left unchecked, they eventually can kill a plant. Lift them off with a cotton swab moistened in rubbing alcohol or spray them with a mixture of equal parts rubbing alcohol and water.

Spider mites usually are found on the undersides of leaves where they spin fine white webs. They suck leaf cells dry, eventually causing leaves to dry and curl. Mites prefer a hot, dry environment, so deter them by misting plants. Regular cleaning of plant leaves and occasional rinsing also can help prevent mites.

Scale insects are smooth, brown, oval pests that look like small shiny bumps. They attach to the undersides of leaves along the midrib or stems. They cause leaf drop, emit sticky secretions, and can kill a plant. Scrape scale off with a fingernail or by wiping with a damp cloth. If scale insects persist, choose an insecticidal soap or horticultural oil that lists them and your plant. Read completely and follow exactly all control agent package directions, including safety warnings.

Thrips usually are found on the undersides of leaves. Using a hand lens, look for small, long-bodied insects with fringed wings. Also inspect for shiny black spots, which are fecal matter. Thrips feed on plant tissue and cause silvering and mottling of stems, foliage, and flowers. They are most active in hot, dry conditions; ward them off by increasing humidity and watering. Soaps and horticultural oil sprays also can be used for large infestations. Again, carefully follow all package directions.

Whiteflies are easy-to-spot, tiny, white, mothlike insects that frequent begonias and herbs. The whitefly larvae and adults suck plant sap and deposit sticky honeydew. Badly infested leaves will yellow and drop. Whiteflies can spread rapidly, so quick detection and treatment are important. Remove and destroy infected plant parts immediately and vacuum up whiteflies at night while they are resting. If necessary, use insecticidal soap following all package instructions. Repeat on a weekly basis until the infestation is under control.

Keep plants healthy by practicing good cultural techniques so they can readily cope with pests.

(Above) Insecticidal soaps have ingredients that include both detergent and ordinary soap, botanical pesticides, and sticking and spreading agents to help them disperse on the plant.

(Below) Sticky traps are a good choice in indoor gardens. They catch flying and small crawling insects that suck or rasp the stems and leaves of your houseplants.

APPLYING INSECTICIDAL SOAP TO HOUSEPLANTS

Insecticidal soaps contain both soap and naturally occurring botanical pesticides, plus other ingredients. Always handle them with the same care reserved for other garden chemicals and wear protective gloves when mixing or applying them to plants. Choose a soap that lists both the specific pest and your houseplant on its label, then read completely and follow exactly the package instructions, using these steps:

1 If the insecticidal soap requires dilution, don rubber gloves and mix it according to the package directions.

2 Insecticidal soaps are effective only if applied directly to the pest; use a cotton-tipped applicator to apply soap to the infested areas.

3 Check leaf undersides and stems for pests and egg clusters. For best results, treat each pest or egg mass.

5 Always properly dispose of empty containers and unused soap solution. Thoroughly wash implements and gloves.

4 After the insecticidal soap has dried, mist the plant with water applied with a hand spray bottle.

INDOOR PLANT DISEASES

Houseplant diseases fall into two main categories—fungal and viral. Most commonly, plants suffer from fungal disease resulting from mildews, molds, and other related organisms. Viral diseases are usually incurable, sometimes are contagious, will affect a plant's vigor and bloom, and can kill it outright. Bacterial infections are another source of disease for houseplants, but they are rarer than either other type.

Although a variety of fungal diseases exist, all cause a plant to mold or rot. They generally result from overwatering or suffocation of roots accompanying compacted soil that lacks sufficient airspace. Common signs of fungal diseases include foliage loss, stunted growth, and droopy leaves. It's easy to mistake wilting as a sign of thirst and apply even more water, exacerbating the problem. In extreme cases, the roots deteriorate, develop fungal infections, and the plant dies. Crown or stem rot is similar. The plant wilts or turns brown, and the plant's stem or trunk becomes soft and discolored near its base. Cure both conditions by cutting back on watering and water only when the soil nears complete dryness. It's important to keep your plants out of standing water and keep their soil loose so that sufficient air reaches their roots. Elevate the plant to allow air penetration to the roots if possible. It may be necessary to repot the plant in a well-draining mix, removing as much of the old soil as possible [see Proper Drainage, pg. 44, and Soils for Planting, pg. 46].

Two fungal conditions commonly occur on foliage. Leaf spot is easy to see. It shows up as soft brown spots on leaves and is common on dieffenbachia and dracaena. The condition usually results from an environment that is too warm, too humid, or poorly ventilated. Prune out affected leaves and dispose of them. Sulfur spray or powder—an organic fungicide—also may be necessary; read completely and follow exactly all package instructions when applying fungicides.

The other fungal disease that often affects foliage is powdery mildew, which appears on plant leaves, stems, and flower buds as a white or gray, dustlike powder. Leaves may curl. Begonias are particularly susceptible. To control powdery mildew, cut off and remove infected plant parts and move the plant to a location with better ventilation, cooler temperatures, and less humidity. Water correctly and avoid overly wet soil [see Watering Houseplants, pg. 68].

Viruses are the other main form of houseplant diseases. Microscopic organisms, they generally affect a certain group of plant species or families of such plants; they are unlikely to spread widely among all of your houseplants. Viruses are often carried by insects such as aphids, mites, and scales, so prompt control of pests is a good step to prevention. Human touch and gardening tools also can spread viruses. People who use tobacco products should wear gloves when handling plants, as their hands may harbor tobacco mosaic virus. Signs of plant virus infections include a lack of vigor, yellow streaking or mottling, and stunted or disfigured growth. Viruses are incurable, so it's best to destroy the infected plant. Before resorting to this course of action, however, isolate the plant and give it proper care to rule out other causes or see if it will recover.

Disease conditions found on houseplants include leaf spot (top), leaf-end blight (second from top), mosaic virus (third from top), and bacterial wilt (bottom). All these conditions can be treated except for the mosaic virus; viral infected plants should be removed from the house and destroyed to avoid spreading the disease.

HOUSEPLANT PEST AND DISEASE SOLUTIONS

Symptom	Cause	Remedies
Curled, twisted, sticky leaves; stunted or deformed blooms; loss of vigor.	Aphids; look for clusters of 1/16-in. (1.6-mm) black, green, yellow, or gray, round insects.	Spray with a stream of water; spray with solution of 2–3 T (30–44 ml) dishwashing liquid per gallon (4 l) of water; spray with insecticidal soap.
White trails on or inside leaves; papery yellow or brown blotches on foliage.	Leaf miners; look for small, pale larvae and 1/6-in. (3.2-mm) tiny green or black flying insects.	Remove infested leaves. Move plant to sheltered outdoor spot and spray foliage with neem oil extract solution.
Stunted plants; white cottony clusters in leaf axils.	Mealybugs; look in the junctions between leaves and stems or at the base of leaf clusters for white or gray, waxy bugs, 1/8 in. (3 mm) long.	Dab or spray with rubbing alcohol diluted 3:1; spray with insecticidal soap; spray with horticultural oil.
Stunted, discolored, spotted plants with deformed roots, sometimes bearing swollen galls; loss of vigor.	Nematodes, microscopic wormlike creatures that live in soil and feed on plant roots.	Repot into sterile potting soil after rinsing roots in neem oil extract solution and pruning away swollen root nodules; may require several repottings at monthly intervals.
Leaves speckle, wrinkle, turn yellow, drop; minute white webs on undersides and the plant's foliage junctions.	Spider mites; shake foliage and blossoms over white paper, and look for moving red or yellow, spiderlike specks. Thrive in hot, dry conditions.	Spray repeatedly with water to rinse off dustlike pests; spray with insecticidal soap.
Stunted, yellow plants lacking vigor; leaves may drop.	Scales; look for 1/20-in. (1.2-mm) flylike insects accompanying soft or hard 1/50-in. (0.5-mm) mounded bumps on stems and leaves.	Remove infested foliage. Swab scales with soapy water or dilute denatured alcohol solution; rinse well after solution dries. Apply horticutural oil. Spray with pyrethrin, rotenone.
Brown-, silver-, or white-speckled leaves; may be gummy or deformed. Blooms are deformed and fail to open.	Thrips; shake foliage and blossoms over white paper, and look for moving winged specks. Thrive in hot, dry conditions.	Remove and destroy infested foliage. Spray with stream of water; spray with insecticidal soap.
Yellow leaves and stunted, sticky plants. When foliage is shaken, a cloud of white insects may fly up.	Whiteflies; shake foliage and look for 1/20-in. (1.2-mm) mothlike flying insects. Inspect leaf undersides for scalelike, gray or yellow eggs.	Catch with sticky traps. Spray with soap solution. Spray infested foliage with insecticidal soap. Move plant to sheltered outdoor spot and spray foliage with horticultural oil or neem oil extract solution. Spray with pyrethrin.
Chewed leaves and blossoms; silvery mucus trails.	Slugs and snails; look after dark on foliage for shelled and unshelled mollusks.	Remove mulch used as hiding places. Hand pick after dark; dust with diatomaceous earth; use nontoxic baits containing iron phosphate; use bait gel.
Brown stains and softened tissue near base of stem or crown of plant; leaves may yellow or drop.	Crown or stem rot; look for decaying stems. Usually associated with keeping soil overly moist.	Rarely curable; remove infected foliage, dipping pruning shears in rubbing alcohol solution between cuts. Reduce watering. Repot to soil-free, well-drained mix. Root cuttings of healthy growth.
Powdery black or brown dusting on foliage and blossoms; leaves may drop.	Leaf spot; fungal disease. Common in low-light, crowded plantings.	Remove shading foliage, increase air circulation; spray with sulfur fungicide.
Light powdery dusting of gray or white on leaves, flowers; deformed new growth; stunting, loss of vigor.	Powdery mildew; fungal disease. Common if humid, warm days and cool nights alternate.	Remove shading foliage, increase air circulation; spray affected plants with solution of 1 T (15 ml) baking soda and 3 T (44 ml) horticultural oil to 1 gallon (4 l) water; dust with sulfur.

ouseplants include a host of bromeliads, bulbs, cacti, ferns, herbs, orchids, palms, shrubs, succulents, trees, and vines that bear colorful flowers, interesting foliage, or both. Choosing from this abundance of fascinating and beautiful plants those that you will treasure and display in your home requires matching their habits and cultural needs with the environmental conditions found in your home.

The 87 plants featured on the following pages include many of the most popular houseplants. Complete descriptions are provided for each plant including its growth habit; flowers; preferred conditions of light, humidity, and temperature; soil and care needs and other features that will help you make your selection. Ideas are given for choosing a room for your plant and integrating it with your decor, and there are tips for special uses.

Use this colorful encyclopedia as a visual identification guide. When you admire houseplants in periodicals, in public buildings, or in your neighbor's home, compare them to the pictures found here and use the information provided to decide whether you should include them in your indoor garden. Each plant is listed by its most common name and its other name variations, then it is listed by its scientific name and family. All the common and scientific names are found in the index. Remember that common names vary regionally—use the scientific name to be sure the plant you acquire is really the one you want.

Encyclopedia of Common Houseplants

Also check the information given for common kitchen herbs that you can grow in your home [see Herbs, pg. 104]. Because many herbs are drought tolerant and enjoy both warmth and bright light, they are easy to grow in window boxes or on sills near your food preparation area. Learn the best herbs to grow to season your salads and prepared dishes.

The encyclopedia of plants that follows is an introduction to the fascinating hobby you will enjoy as you begin your indoor garden. The pleasure houseplants bring will be a reflection of the love and care you give to these lovely, living additions to your life and home.

(Clockwise from upper left) Start an exploration of the fascinating world of houseplants with these four popular choices: Elephant's-ear; fancy-leaved caladium; Alocasia sanderiana, *a flamingo flower relative; and red vase plant, a colorful bromeliad.*

Name: African Violet. *Saintpaulia* species. GESNERIACEAE.

Description: About 21 species and many cultivars of fast-growing, low and mounding, perennial herbs, 3–16 in. (75–400 mm) tall. Deep green or variegated, fuzzy, oval or lance-shaped leaves, 1½–3½ in. (38–90 mm) long, in flat rosettes. Clusters of single, semi-double, or double, sometimes ruffled or fringed, usually blue, violet, white, sometimes bicolored flowers, ½–2 in. (12–50 mm) wide, with yellow, ball-shaped anthers. Spring–autumn blooming. *S. ionantha* is commonly cultivated. Dwarf, trailing cultivars available.

Conditions: Light: filtered sun, 4–6 hours daily. Humidity: 60–80%. Temperature: 60–75°F (16–24°C).

Soil: Well-drained, rich. 6.0–6.5 pH.

Care: Moderate–challenging. Water when soil surface dries, avoiding foliage. Mass several plants in a stone-filled cachepot to add humidity. Fertilize with each watering; dilute liquid fertilizer to half its recommended rate. Deadhead flower clusters at stem base. Repot in spring if crowded. Propagate by leaf and stem cuttings, division, seed.

Features: Good choice for tables, windowsills in bathrooms. Aphid, mealybug, spider mite and brown spot, crown rot susceptible.

Name: Aloe, Medicinal; Medicine Plant. *Aloe vera (A. barbadensis)*. LILIACEAE.

Description: Slow-growing, upright, succulent, perennial herb, to 2 ft. (60 cm) tall. Fleshy, medium green, narrow, lance-shaped, sharp-toothed leaves, 1–2 ft. (30–60 cm) long, clustered in rosettes. Clusters of yellow flowers, to 1 in. (25 mm) long, on stalks to 3 ft. (90 cm) tall. Summer blooming.

Conditions: Light: full sun, 6–8 hours daily. Humidity: 20–40%. Temperature: 65–80°F. (18–27°C).

Soil: Well-drained, average. 7.0–8.0 pH.

Care: Easy. Water only after soil dries. Fertilize quarterly spring–autumn. Deadhead flowers and withered stalks. Prune only withered leaves. Repot if very crowded. Propagate by cuttings, seed.

Features: Good choice for tables, plant stands in cactus groups, sitting rooms, solariums. Mix with other arid succulents for interesting-textured plantings. Sap is source of medicinal aloe used to treat burns, skin irritation. Pest and disease resistant.

Name: Aluminum Plant. *Pilea cadierei*. URTICACEAE.

Description: Fast-growing, mounding, succulent perennial herb, to 1 ft. (30 cm) tall. Textured, green-and-silver-patterned, oval, lightly toothed leaves, to 3 in. (75 mm) long. Insignificant flowers. *P. cadierei* 'Minima' is a dwarf cultivar.

Conditions: Light: filtered sun, 4–6 hours daily. Humidity: 70–90%. Temperature: 65–85°F (18–29°C).

Soil: Well-drained, rich–average. 6.5–7.5 pH.

Care: Easy. Water when soil surface dries. Fertilize monthly spring–autumn. Pinch or prune frequently for dense foliage. Avoid repotting; in spring root new plants. Propagate by stem cuttings.

Features: Good choice for hanging baskets, tables, terrariums in sitting rooms. Mealybug, spider mite susceptible.

Name: Amaryllis, Florist's. *Hippeastrum* hybrids. AMARYLLIDACEAE.

Description: About 80 species and many hybrids of deciduous or evergreen tropical bulbs, 8–24 in. (20–60 cm) tall. Broad, straplike, medium green, arching, broad, pointed leaves, to 18 in. (45 cm) long. One to five orange, pink, red, white, sometimes bicolored, flared, trumpet-shaped flowers, 5–10 in. (13–25 cm) wide, on tall, single or double stalks. Spring blooming or forced.

Conditions: Light: full to partial sun, 5–8 hours daily. Humidity: 50–80%. Temperature: 60–80°F (16–27°C).

Soil: Well-drained, rich. 6.0–6.5 pH.

Care: Easy. Water thoroughly at planting, thereafter when soil surface dries. Withhold water for 4–6 weeks in late summer to force dormancy. Fertilize bimonthly during growth. Stake to support flower stalks. Deadhead flowers and withered stalks; set outdoors in a sunny spot protected from frost. Repot in autumn. Propagate by offsets, seed.

Features: Good choice for tables in sitting rooms, solariums. Good for cutting, forcing, massed plantings. Mass several bulbs in a large, flat container. Good garden gift. Pest and disease resistant. Slug, snail susceptible.

Name: Arrowhead Vine; Nephthytis. *Syngonium podophyllum.* ARACEAE.

Description: Fast-growing, perennial, tropical evergreen vine, to 6 ft. (1.8 m) tall. Smooth, shiny, green, pink, silver, and white, variegated, 3–10-lobed, pointed leaves, to 1 ft. (30 cm) long. Flowers rare; grown primarily for foliage.

Conditions: Light: filtered or indirect sun, 4–6 hours daily. Humidity: 40–70%. Temperature: 60–75°F (16–24°C).

Soil: Well-drained, rich–average. 6.5–7.5 pH.

Care: Easy. Water when soil surface dries. Fertilize semi-monthly until plant attains desired size, quarterly thereafter. Turn frequently. Stake on fibrous pole to support tendrils, or allow to trail. Prune sparingly. Repot in spring if crowded. Propagate by stem cuttings, layering.

Features: Good choice for hanging baskets, floors, ledges, tables in bathrooms, bedrooms, sitting rooms. Mealybug, spider mite susceptible.

Name: Asparagus Fern; Lace Fern. *Asparagus setaceus (A. plumosus).* LILIACEAE.

Description: Slow-growing, branching perennial, evergreen vining shrub, to 4 ft. (1.2 m) wide. Feathery, fernlike green foliage, to 6 in. (15 cm) long, in delicate sprays on wirelike stems. Inconspicuous flowers develop purple berries. *A. setaceus* 'Nanus' is a dwarf cultivar. Emerald fern, *A. densiflorus* 'Sprengeri', is a commonly cultivated relative.

Conditions: Light: filtered sun, 4–6 hours daily. Humidity: 50–80%. Temperature: 55–75°F (13–24°C).

Soil: Well-drained, rich. 6.0–7.0 pH.

Care: Easy. Water when soil surface dries; water sparingly in winter. Mist occasionally. Fertilize bimonthly; dilute liquid fertilizer to half its recommended rate. Prune sparingly. Repot in spring if crowded, or top dress with a layer of fresh soil, 1 in. (25 mm) thick. Propagate by cuttings, division, seed.

Features: Good choice for hanging baskets, ledges, tables in bathrooms, kitchens. Good for cutting, training onto windows. Fungal disease susceptible.

Name: Avocado; Alligator Pear. *Persea americana.* LAURACEAE.

Description: Slow-growing, upright, open and very branching, woody, tropical evergreen tree, to over 60 ft. (18.3 m) tall outdoors, but indoors rarely over 5 ft. (1.5 m). Smoothly textured, dull, deep green, oval and pointed leaves, 4–8 in. (10–20 cm) long, in groups of 3–5 per stem. Insignificant flowers.

Conditions: Light: full to partial sun, 6–8 hours daily. Humidity: 40–70%. Temperature: 55–80°F (13–27°C).

Soil: Well-drained, average. 6.0–7.5 pH.

Care: Easy. Water when soil surface dries. Fertilize semi-monthly spring–autumn. Prune sparingly. Repot annually in spring. Propagate by cuttings, seed. Sprout large seed suspended in water, blunt end down as with hyacinth, at 65°F (18°C) until shoot appears, then pot into soil.

Features: Good choice for floors, plant stands, windowsills in kitchens, solariums. Good project for children. Pest and disease resistant.

Name: Banana; Plantain. *Musa* species. MUSACEAE.

Description: About 25 species of fast-growing, treelike, spreading, tropical rhizomatous herbs, to over 15 ft. (4.6 m) tall outdoors, but indoors rarely over 5 ft. (1.5 m). Smooth, shiny, light green, sometimes striped with brown or purple, broad-bladed fronds, to 5 ft. (1.5 m) long, from trunklike base. Yellow flowers grow from center of leaf stalks on a stem bearing red or purple bracts, forming edible or inedible fruits in fingerlike clusters.

Conditions: Light: full to filtered sun, 6–8 hours daily. Humidity: 70–90%. Temperature: 65–85°F (18–29°C).

Soil: Well-drained, very rich. 6.0–7.0 pH.

Care: Moderate–challenging. Water to keep soil evenly moist. Fertilize monthly. Mist regularly. Prune fruited stalks to soil. Repot semi-annually in spring; top dress annually with a layer of fresh soil, 1–2 in. (25–50 mm) thick. Propagate by division, offsets, seed.

Features: Good choice for landings and floors in bathrooms, entries, sitting rooms, solariums. Good for tropical effects. Aphid, mealybug, spider mite, and brown spot susceptible.

Name: Beef Plant; Beefsteak Plant; Bloodleaf. *Iresine herbstii.* AMARANTHACEAE.

Description: Many cultivars of moderate-growing, mounding or trailing, dense, perennial herb, 18–32 in. (45–80 cm) tall. Smooth, waxy, purple, red, yellow, usually variegated, oval, wavy, veined and notch-tipped leaves, to 5 in. (13 cm) long. Flowers inconspicuous; grown primarily for colorful foliage.

Conditions: Light: full to filtered sun, 3–5 hours daily. Humidity: 40–70%. Temperature: 65–75°F (18–24°C).

Soil: Well-drained, rich. 6.5–7.5 pH.

Care: Easy. Water when soil surface dries; reduce watering in winter. Fertilize quarterly spring–summer. Pinch growth tips to promote fullness. Avoid pruning. Repot annually; in third season, replace. Propagate by stem cuttings.

Features: Good choice for hanging baskets, ledges, terrariums in entries, sitting rooms. Good for color. Plant cuttings outdoors as an annual for unusual foliage color. Fungal disease resistant. Aphid, mealybug, thrip susceptible.

Name: Begonia, Rex. *Begonia* × *rex-cultorum* hybrids. BEGONIACEAE.

Description: Many cultivars and hybrids of fast-growing, mounding or trailing rhizomatous herbs with varied habits, 6–12 in. (15–30 cm) tall and 1–3 ft. (30–90 cm) wide. Textured, heart-shaped, brown, green, pink, white, yellow, always colorfully variegated, toothed leaves, 6–12 in. (15–30 cm) long, on fuzzy leaf stalks. Flowers inconspicuous; grown primarily for colorful foliage. Some hybrids dormant in winter. King or painted-leaf begonia, *B. rex*, the progenitor of its many hybrids, is rarely found in cultivation as a pure species.

Conditions: Light: partial shade. Humidity: 50–80%. Temperature: 60–80°F (16–27°C).

Soil: Well-drained, rich. 5.5–6.5 pH.

Care: Moderate–challenging. Water only when soil surface dries; water sparingly in winter. Fertilize bimonthly spring–summer. Mist frequently or place plant on stones over water in cachepot. Prune sparingly. Pinch growth tips to promote fullness. Repot in 2–3 years or when very crowded. Propagate by cuttings, division.

Features: Good choice for floors, ledges, tables in entries, halls, landings. Good for color. Powdery mildew susceptible.

Name: Begonia, Tuberous. *Begonia* × *tuberhybrida* hybrids. BEGONIACEAE.

Description: Many hybrids of fast-growing, erect, mounding or trailing deciduous tubers, 1–3 ft. (30–90 cm) tall or long. Smooth, shiny, brittle, wing-shaped, bronze green leaves, to 6 in. (15 cm) long, with reddish veins. Multiple orange, pink, red, rose, yellow, variegated, single, double, or very double flowers, 2–6 in. (50–150 mm) wide, sometimes fringed or ruffled. Summer- or autumn-blooming. Dormant in winter.

Conditions: Light: indirect sun, 4–6 hours daily. Humidity: 60–80%. Temperature: 60–70°F (16–21°C) during growth; store lifted tubers in dark in net bag or open basket of dry peat moss, 40–50°F (4–10°C).

Soil: Well-drained, rich. 5.5–6.5 pH.

Care: Moderate. Water to keep soil evenly moist during growth; reduce watering in winter. Fertilize at alternate waterings; dilute liquid fertilizer to half its recommended rate. Protect from heat. Deadhead spent flowers. Cut back and lift in autumn. Repot annually in early spring. Propagate by stem cuttings, division, seed.

Features: Good choice for hanging baskets, ledges, plant stands, tables in bathrooms, kitchens, sitting rooms, solariums. Slug, snail susceptible.

Name: Begonia, Wax. *Begonia* × *semperflorens-cultorum* hybrids. BEGONIACEAE.

Description: Many cultivars of fast-growing, upright, bushy, succulent, fibrous-rooted, half-hardy perennial herbs, 8–12 in. (20–30 cm) tall. Waxy, pink, red, white single flowers, to 1 in. (25 mm) wide. Smooth, shiny, bronze, green, red, white, variegated leaves, to 1 in. (25 mm) wide. Spring–autumn blooming. Angel wing begonia, *B. coccinea*, is a close relative with many attractive cultivars.

Conditions: Light: partial shade. Humidity: 40–60%. Temperature: 60–85°F (16–29°C).

Soil: Well-drained, rich. 7.0 pH.

Care: Easy. Water to keep soil evenly moist. Fertilize monthly spring–autumn. Pinch growth tips to promote fullness. Repot annually. Propagate by stem cuttings, seed.

Features: Good choice for hanging baskets, ledges, windowsills in bedrooms, halls, sitting rooms. Whitefly, mealybug, and leaf spot susceptible.

Name: Bird-of-Paradise. *Strelitzia reginae.* STRELITZIACEAE.
Description: Fast-growing, branching, woody tropical herb, to 4 ft.
(1.2 m) tall. Smooth, shiny, palmlike, green, broadly lance-shaped
leaves, to 18 in. (45 cm) long, on upright stems. Unusual, birdlike, blue, orange,
and white, crested flowers, to 1 ft. (30 cm) long, only on mature plants 4–6 years old.
Intermittent year-round blooming.
Conditions: Light: full sun, 8–10 hours daily. Humidity:
40–70%. Temperature: 50–80°F (10–27°C).
Soil: Well-drained, rich. 6.0–7.0 pH.
Care: Moderate–challenging. Water when soil surface dries; reduce
watering in winter. Mist occasionally. Fertilize bimonthly. Deadhead spent flowers,
yellowed foliage. Repot annually in spring until mature; top dress thereafter with a layer
of fresh soil, 1 in. (25 mm) thick. Propagate by division, seed, suckers.
Features: Good choice for floors in sitting rooms, solariums. Good for cutting.
Pest and disease resistant.

Name: Burro's-Tail; Donkey's-Tail. *Sedum morganianum.* CRASSULACEAE.
Description: Slow-growing, branching and trailing, succulent perennial
herb, to 3 ft. (90 cm) tall. Smooth, brittle, fleshy, succulent, tear-
shaped, light green leaves, to 1 in. (25 mm) long, cascade
from ropelike stalks, 3–4 ft. (90–120 cm) long. Pink, yellow
flowers, to ½ in. (12 mm) long, are rare; grown primarily for
unusual foliage.
Conditions: Light: full sun, 5–8 hours daily. Humidity: 20–50%. Temperature:
60–75°F (16–24°C).
Soil: Well-drained, sandy, rich. 7.0–8.0 pH.
Care: Easy–moderate. Water only after soil dries; reduce watering in winter. Fertilize
quarterly spring–autumn. Prune sparingly; protect brittle foliage stalks from movement.
Repot in spring. Propagate by leaf cuttings.
Features: Good choice for hanging baskets, ledges in low-traffic areas. Pest and disease resistant.

Name: Cactus, Barrel; Golden-Ball Cactus. *Echinocactus grusonii.* CACTACEAE.
Description: Slow-growing, round, spiny cactus, to 3 ft. (90 cm) tall and wide outdoors, but
indoors rarely over 1 ft. (30 cm) tall. Armed with sharp, stiff, golden yellow turning brown,
hook-free spines, to 2 in. (50 mm) long, in radiating, overlapping clusters beneath a
woolly top. Tubular yellow flowers, to 2½ in. (65 mm) long, ring the cactus's top.
Summer blooming. *E. horizonthalonius*, with pink flowers, is a closely related species, as
are members of the genera *Echinocereus*, with similar care needs.
Conditions: Light: full sun, 6–8 hours daily. Humidity: 10–40%. Temperature:
50–85°F (10–29°C) spring–autumn, 35–50°F (2–10°C) winter.
Soil: Well-drained, sandy, average. 7.0–8.5 pH.
Care: Easy. Water only after soil completely dries. Fertilize quarterly spring–autumn.
Repot if crowded; top dress annually with a layer of fresh soil, ½ in. (12 mm) thick.
Propagate by offsets, seed.
Features: Good choice for ledges, windowsills in cactus and succulent groups, sitting
rooms, solariums. Good for southwestern regional flair. Mealybug, scale, and fungal
disease susceptible.

Name: Cactus, Easter. *Rhipsalidopsis gaertneri (Hatiora gaertneri).* CACTACEAE.
Description: Moderate-growing, jointed, trailing, tropical, epiphytic cactus, to 16 in. (40 cm) wide. Smooth, fleshy, deep green, flattened, scalloped, segmented stems, to 8 in. (20 cm) long, armed with bristles. Clusters of bright red, many-pointed petals form flared, double flowers, to 3½ in. (90 mm) long. Spring blooming; may repeat in autumn. Semi-dormant September–March.
Conditions: Light: filtered sun, 6–8 hours daily. Humidity: 70–90%. Temperature: indoors 55–60°F (13–16°C) September–March, then 60–75°F (16–24°C) April–May; outdoors 60–85°F (16–29°C) June–September.
Soil: Well-drained, sandy, rich. 6.0–7.0 pH.
Care: Moderate–challenging. Water to keep soil evenly moist during growth; limit watering September–March. Mist frequently. Fertilize with each watering during growth. Rest and outdoor exposure necessary for flowering. Prune sparingly. Repot only if very crowded. Propagate by stem cuttings, division, seed.
Features: Good choice for hanging baskets, ledges, plant stands, tables in bathrooms, kitchens, solariums. Slug, snail susceptible.

Name: Cactus, Old-Man. *Cephalocereus senilis.* CACTACEAE.
Description: Very slow growing, columnar, ribbed, subtropical cactus, to 50 ft. (15 m) tall outdoors, but indoors rarely over 16 in. (40 cm). Armed with sharp, stiff, yellow spines, to 1½ in. (38 mm) long, in clusters hidden beneath massed, woolly, gray, hairlike bristles, to 1 ft. (30 cm) long. Pink, oval flowers, to 2 in. (50 mm) long, are rare indoors; night blooming in spring. Grown primarily for its unique foliage.
Conditions: Light: full sun, 6–8 hours daily. Humidity: 40–60%. Temperature: 35–80°F (2–27°C).
Soil: Well-drained, sandy, average. 6.5–8.0 pH.
Care: Easy. Water only after soil completely dries. Fertilize with each watering spring–autumn; dilute liquid fertilizer to half its recommended rate. Avoid pruning. Repot when roots become compacted. Propagate by stem cuttings, seed.
Features: Good choice for tables in entries, halls, bright rooms, solariums. Good for southwest regional flair. Mealybug, scale, and fungal disease susceptible.

Name: Cactus, Orchid. *Epiphyllum ackermannii* × *epicactus (Nopalxochia ackermanni).* CACTACEAE.
Description: Moderate-growing, arching, trailing, tropical, epiphytic cactus, to 2 ft. (60 cm) tall. Smooth, fleshy, deep green, flattened, notched stems, to 16 in. (40 cm) long, with few bristly spines. Red, many-pointed petals form showy, flared, waxy flowers, to 7 in. (18 cm) wide. Late-spring blooming. Semi-dormant December–March.
Conditions: Light: filtered sun, 6–8 hours daily. Humidity: 70–90%. Temperature: indoors 60–75°F (16–24°C) October–November, 40–50°F (4–10°C) December–April, then 60–75°F (16–24°C) May–June; outdoors 60–85°F (16–29°C) July–September.
Soil: Well-drained, sandy, rich. 6.0–7.0 pH.
Care: Moderate–challenging. Water when soil surface dries; limit watering December–April. Mist frequently. Fertilize monthly during growth. Stake to support stems. Rest and outdoor exposure necessary for flowering. Prune sparingly. Repot only if very crowded. Propagate by cuttings, seed.
Features: Good choice for hanging baskets, tables, ledges, plant stands in bathrooms, kitchens, solariums. Slug, snail susceptible.

Name: Cactus, Snowball; Powder-Puff Cactus. *Mammillaria bocasana.* CACTACEAE.

Description: Very slow growing, subtropical cactus, to 8 in. (20 cm) tall. Smooth, bluish green, round, clustered stems, to 6 in. (15 cm) long, armed with sharp, white, yellow, hooked spines, in interlocking clusters beneath woolly, silver, hairlike bristles. Yellow, oval flowers, to ¾ in. (19 mm) long, ring the cactus's top. Summer blooming. Semi-dormant in winter.

Conditions: Light: full sun, 6–8 hours daily. Humidity: 10–50%. Temperature: 35–50°F (2–10°C) November–February, then 60–85°F (16–29°C) March–October.

Soil: Well-drained, sandy, average. 7.0–8.0 pH.

Care: Easy. Water only after soil completely dries; withhold water in winter. Fertilize quarterly spring–autumn. Winter rest necessary for flowering. Avoid pruning. Repot when roots become compacted. Propagate by cuttings, division, seed.

Features: Good choice for arid terrariums, tables, ledges in entries, halls, sitting rooms. Mealybug, scale, and fungal disease susceptible.

Name: Caladium, Fancy-Leaved; Angel-Wings; Elephant's-Ear. *Caladium x hortulanum (C. bicolor).* ARACEAE.

Description: Fast-growing, spreading, deciduous, perennial tuber, 2–3 ft. (60–90 cm) tall. Smooth, shiny, ribbed, heart-shaped, light green leaves, to 18 in. (45 cm) long, with showy pink, red, and white variegated patterns. Flowers insignificant; grown for foliage.

Conditions: Light: indirect sun or partial shade. Humidity: 60–80%. Temperature: 60–80°F (16–27°C) during growth; store lifted tubers in dark in net bag or open basket of dry peat moss, 50–60°F (10–16°C).

Soil: Well-drained, rich. 5.5–6.5 pH.

Care: Moderate. Water thoroughly at planting, thereafter when soil surface dries; withhold water 4–6 weeks in October to force dormancy. Fertilize during growth. Cut back foliage and lift in autumn, store; repot annually in spring. Propagate by offsets.

Features: Good choice for hanging baskets, plant stands in bathrooms, kitchens, landings, low-light rooms. Pest and disease resistant.

Name: Cast-Iron Plant. *Aspidistra elatior* 'Variegata' *(A. lurida).* LILIACEAE.

Description: Moderate-growing, spreading, perennial, rhizomatous, evergreen herb, to 2 ft. (60 cm) tall. Leathery or glossy, oblong, green-and-white-striped, pointed leaves, to 2½ ft. (75 cm) long, from rolled basal sheaths. Inconspicuous flowers.

Conditions: Light: filtered or indirect sun, 4–6 hours daily. Humidity: 30–70%. Temperature: 45–70°F (7–21°C).

Soil: Well-drained, average. 6.5–7.5 pH.

Care: Easy. Water when soil surface dries; reduce watering in winter. Mist occasionally. Fertilize quarterly spring–autumn. Tolerant of intermittent care. Prune sparingly. Trim brown leaf tips with scissors. Avoid repotting. Propagate by division in spring.

Features: Good choice for hanging baskets, floors, ledges, tables in bathrooms, bedrooms, entries, low-light rooms. Pest resistant. Crown rot susceptible if overwatered.

Name: Chinese Evergreen. *Aglaonema modestum* 'Silver Queen'. ARACEAE.

Description: Slow-growing, mounding, perennial, rhizomatous, tropical herb, to 3 ft. (90 cm) tall. Leathery, lance-shaped, gray, green, white, silver, variegated, veined, pointed leaves, to 8 in. (20 cm) long. Green, callalike flowers, to 4 in. (10 cm) long, form orange, berrylike fruits. Spring blooming. Grown primarily for showy foliage. Deep green *A.* x *modestum* hybrids available.

Conditions: Light: filtered sun to full shade. Humidity: 50–80%. Temperature: 60–75°F (16–24°C).

Soil: Well-drained, average. 6.0–7.0 pH.

Care: Easy. Water to keep soil evenly moist during growth; water sparingly in winter. Fertilize monthly spring–autumn. Prune sparingly. Repot when roots become compacted. Propagate by stem cuttings, division, seed.

Features: Good choice for floors, ledges, tables in bathrooms, halls, low-light rooms. Good for massed plantings. Aphid, mealybug, spider mite, and air pollution susceptible.

Name: Citrus (Grapefruit, Lemon, Lime, Orange). *Citrus* species. RUTACEAE.

Description: About 16 species of branching, spiny, fruiting, evergreen shrubs and trees, to over 30 ft. (9.2 m) outdoors, but indoors rarely over 6 ft. (1.8 m). Smooth, shiny, deep green, oval, pointed leaves, to 4 in. (10 cm) long. Purple, white, star-shaped, very fragrant flowers, 1–2 in. (25–50 mm) wide, form edible and inedible segmented, juicy fruits. Spring or year-round blooming, depending on species and cultivar. Choose dwarf cultivars for indoor use.

Conditions: Light: full sun, 6–10 hours daily. Humidity: 30–70%. Temperature: 70–90°F (21–32°C) spring–autumn, 45–60°F (7–16°C) winter.

Soil: Well-drained, rich–average. 6.0–6.5 pH.

Care: Easy–moderate. Water when soil surface dries; water sparingly in winter. Fertilize bimonthly with acid organic fertilizer containing micronutrients: calcium, iron, zinc, manganese. Pollinate using an artist's brush. Prune sparingly. Move outdoors in summer. Repot in spring if crowded; top dress annually with a layer of fresh soil, 1 in. (25 mm) thick. Propagate by cuttings, grafting, seed.

Features: Good choice for floors, groups in full-sun locations. Good for fruit. Aphid, mealybug, spider mite, scale, and iron chlorosis susceptible.

Name: Coleus; Flame Nettle; Painted Leaf Plant; Painted Nettle. *Solenostemon scutellariodes* (*Coleus* x *hybridus*). LABIATAE.

Description: Many cultivars of upright, shrublike, tender perennial, tropical herbs, to 7 ft. (2.1 m) outdoors, but indoors rarely over 2 ft. (60 cm). Textured, green, orange, pink, red, white, yellow, variegated, heart- or dagger-shaped, saw-edged leaves, 3–7 in. (75–175 mm) long, radiating from multiple square stems. Nettlelike, blue, violet flowers insignificant; grown primarily for colorful foliage.

Conditions: Light: filtered sun, 6–8 hours daily. Humidity: 60–80%. Temperature: 50–85°F (10–29°C).

Soil: Well-drained, rich. 7.0–7.5 pH.

Care: Moderate. Water to keep soil evenly moist. Mist frequently. Fertilize with each watering; dilute liquid fertilizer to half its recommended rate. Deadhead flower buds. Pinch frequently to promote fullness. Avoid repotting; in spring, seed new plants. Propagate by stem cuttings, seed.

Features: Good choice for hanging baskets, ledges, plant stands in bathrooms, bedrooms, halls, low-light rooms. Good for color, massed plantings. Aphid susceptible.

Name: Corn Plant. *Dracaena fragrans* 'Massangeana'. AGAVACEAE.
Description: Slow-growing, upright, perennial, evergreen, tropical, palmlike false palm, to 20 ft. (6 m) tall outdoors, but indoors rarely over 8 ft. (2.4 m). Shiny, sword-shaped, green-and-yellow-striped, narrow, pointed leaves, to 3 ft. (90 cm) long and 4 in. (10 cm) wide. Creamy flowers rare; grown for foliage. A related species, *D. deremensis* 'Janet Craig', with solid green foliage, is smaller in size and similar in form. Plants of the family *Cordyline* sometimes are confused with *Dracaena* species.
Conditions: Light: full or indirect sun, 3–4 hours daily. Humidity: 50–70%. Temperature: 60–75°F (16–24°C).
Soil: Well-drained, sandy, average. 6.5–7.5 pH.
Care: Easy. Water when soil surface dries. Mist and wipe foliage occasionally. Fertilize annually in spring. Prune sparingly. Trim brown leaf tips with scissors. Repot when roots become compacted. Propagate by stem cuttings, layering.
Features: Good choice for floors, landings in low-light and tall-ceilinged rooms, solariums. Good for tropical effects. Recent transplants may have limited root systems. Pest and disease resistant.

Name: Crocus. *Crocus* species. IRIDACEAE.
Description: About 80 species of deciduous corms, 3–6 in. (75–150 mm) tall. Shiny, grasslike, deep green leaves, to 6 in. (15 cm) long. Purple, white, yellow, sometimes striped, single, cup-shaped, sometimes fragrant flowers, 1½–3 in. (38–75 mm) long, appear stemless. Spring or autumn blooming.
Conditions: Light: full sun, 4–6 hours daily. Humidity: 40–70%. Temperature: 50–60°F (10–16°C) during growth; store lifted corms in dark in net bag or open basket of dry peat moss, 40–50°F (4–10°C). Chill after autumn planting 14–16 weeks, 35–40°F (2–4°C).
Soil: Well-drained, rich. 5.0–6.5 pH.
Care: Easy. Water to keep soil evenly moist during growth; water sparingly during chilling. Fertilize only at planting. When sprouts emerge after chilling, move to display location for growth, bloom. Lift after flowering, store; plant outdoors in autumn. Propagate by division, seed.
Features: Good choice for tables in cool kitchens, bathrooms, dining rooms. Good for color, forcing. Pest and disease resistant.

Name: Croton, Florist's; Variegated Laurel. *Codiaeum* species. EUPHORBIACEAE.
Description: About six species of moderate-growing, upright, tropical, evergreen shrubs, 3–4 ft. (90–120 cm) tall. Showy, waxy or leathery, green, red, white, yellow, variegated, veined, sometimes lobed leaves, to 1 ft. (30 cm) long. White flowers rare; grown for colorful foliage. Hybrids of 'Joseph's Coat', *C. variegatum* var. *pictum*, are most common cultivars.
Conditions: Light: full sun, 6–8 hours daily. Humidity: 70–90%. Temperature: 65–80°F (18–27°C); avoid exposure to temperatures cooler than 60°F (16°C).
Soil: Well-drained, rich. 6.5–7.5 pH.
Care: Moderate–challenging. Water to keep soil evenly moist spring–autumn; water sparingly in winter. Fertilize monthly during growth. Changes to temperature, light causes foliage drop. Avoid pruning or repotting. Propagate by stem cuttings, layering, seed.
Features: Good choice for floors, landings in bathrooms, solariums. Good for color. Avoid hazard to clothing and implements from permanent, staining sap. Aphid, mealybug, leaf miner, scale, thrip susceptible.

Name: Cyclamen, Florist's; Persian Violet. *Cyclamen persicum.* PRIMULACEAE.

Description: Many cultivars of mounding, perennial tubers, 6–12 in. (15–30 cm) tall. Shiny, heart-shaped, green, white, silver, variegated leaves, to 5½ in. (14 cm) long and wide. Pink, purple, red, white, bicolored, winged, sometimes frilled, often fragrant flowers, to 2 in. (50 mm) long, on tall, slender stalks. Winter–spring blooming. Semi-dormant in summer. Dwarf cultivars available.

Conditions: Light: indirect sun, 6–8 hours daily. Humidity: 60–80%. Temperature: 50–60°F (10–16°C) during growth; store lifted tubers in dark in pot of dry–slightly damp soil, 60–70°F (16–21°C).

Soil: Well-drained, rich. 6.0–6.5 pH.

Care: Easy. Water to keep soil evenly moist autumn–spring. Fertilize monthly until bloom; dilute liquid fertilizer to half its recommended rate. Stop watering after flowers fade. Once dormant, store pot; repot in autumn. Propagate by division, seed.

Features: Good choice for tables in cool rooms, dining rooms. Good for color, forcing. Pest and disease resistant.

Name: Dragon Tree. *Draceaena draco.* AGAVACEAE.

Description: Slow-growing, upright, perennial, evergreen, tropical, yuccalike false palm, to 20 ft. (6 m) tall outdoors, but indoors rarely over 6 ft. (1.8 m). Leathery, sword-shaped, deep green, narrow, pointed leaves, to 2 ft. (60 cm) long, in bunched clusters atop sinuous branches. Green flowers rare; grown for foliage and graceful form. A related species, *D. marginata*, with narrow, branching stems, bears red-, yellow-, purple-fringed and striped leaves.

Conditions: Light: full or indirect sun, 3–4 hours daily. Humidity: 40–60%. Temperature: 60–75°F (16–24°C).

Soil: Well-drained, sandy, average. 6.5–7.5 pH.

Care: Easy. Water when soil surface dries. Mist and wipe foliage occasionally. Fertilize annually in spring. Prune sparingly. Repot when roots become too compacted. Propagate by stem cuttings, layering.

Features: Good choice for floors, landings, solariums in low-light and tall-ceilinged rooms. Recent transplants may have limited root systems. Pest and disease resistant.

Name: Dumb Cane; Tuftroot. *Dieffenbachia* hybrids. ARACEAE.

Description: Many hybrids and cultivars of fast- and moderate-growing, upright, spreading, perennial, tropical, evergreen herbs, to 5 ft. (1.5 m) tall. Smooth, shiny, broadly oblong, green, white, yellow, variegated leaves, to 1 ft. (30 cm) long, on flaring stems. Flared, green, narrow, callalike flowers, to 4 in. (10 cm) long.

Conditions: Light: filtered or indirect sun, 4–6 hours daily. Humidity: 50–70%. Temperature: 60–80°F (16–27°C).

Soil: Well-drained, rich–average. 6.0–7.0 pH.

Care: Easy. Water when soil surface dries; reduce watering in winter. Mist frequently. Fertilize bimonthly spring–autumn; dilute liquid fertilizer to half its recommended rate. Prune foliage to crown when leggy; plant will resprout. Repot annually in spring. Propagate by crown, leaf, stem cuttings, division.

Features: Good choice for floors, ledges, tables in bathrooms, kitchens, solariums. Mealybug, spider mite, scale susceptible.

Warning

Sap of dumb cane is hazardous if ingested. Avoid use in households frequented by children or pets.

Name: Fatsia, Japanese; Castor-Oil Plant. *Fatsia japonica (Aralia sieboldii)*. ARALIACEAE.
Description: Moderate-growing, branching, upright, deciduous or evergreen shrub, to 20 ft. (6 m) tall outdoors, but indoors rarely over 10 ft. (3 m). Smooth, shiny, figlike, green, white, yellow, seven-lobed leaves, to 1 ft. (30 cm) wide. Cream and yellow flower clusters rare; grown primarily for foliage.
Conditions: Light: filtered sun to partial shade. Humidity: 40–70%. Temperature: 50–65°F (10–18°C) spring–autumn, 45–50°F (7–10°C) winter.
Soil: Well-drained, average–low. 6.5–7.5 pH.
Care: Easy. Water when soil surface dries; reduce watering in winter. Fertilize bimonthly; dilute liquid fertilizer to half its recommended rate. Prune growth tips in spring to promote fullness. Repot annually in spring until plant reaches desired size; top dress annually thereafter. Propagate by stem cuttings, seed.
Features: Good choice for floors, landings in cool, low-light rooms, entries. Good for tropical effects. Aphid, mealybug, spider mite, scale susceptible.

Name: Fern, Bird's-Nest; Nest Fern. *Asplenium nidus.* POLYPODIACEAE.
Description: Slow-growing, spreading, tropical, rhizomatous, evergreen, epiphytic fern, to 3 ft. (90 cm) tall. Shiny, spear-shaped, light green, ribbed, slightly scalloped, solid fronds, to 2 ft. (60 cm) long, on fibrous-based leaf stalks. Grown for foliage.
Conditions: Light: indirect sun, 4–6 hours daily. Humidity: 50–80%. Temperature: 55–70°F (13–21°C).
Soil: Well-drained, sandy, average–low. 5.5–6.5 pH.
Care: Moderate. Water to keep soil evenly moist; avoid wetting foliage. Mist frequently. Place in a stone-filled cachepot to add humidity. Fertilize monthly; dilute liquid fertilizer to half its recommended strength. Avoid contact with tender young fronds. Prune to remove all dead, broken fronds. Repot when roots emerge from soil. Propagate by division, spores.
Features: Good choice for plant stands, tables in bathrooms, kitchens. Mealybug, scale, spider mite susceptible.

Name: Fern, Boston. *Nephrolepis exaltata* 'Bostoniensis'. POLYPODIACEAE.
Description: Many cultivars of moderate-growing, arching or mounding, perennial, rhizomatous, evergreen fern, to 3 ft. (90 cm) tall. Smooth, spear-shaped, deep green, narrow, pointed fronds, to 4 ft. (1.2 m) long, with segmented leaflets and often bearing stoloniferous runners on fibrous-based leaf stalks. Grown for foliage.
Conditions: Light: indirect sun, 4–6 hours daily. Humidity: 50–80%. Temperature: 60–70°F (16–21°C).
Soil: Well-drained, rich. 6.0–7.0 pH.
Care: Easy. Water to keep soil evenly moist. Mist frequently. Fertilize monthly; dilute liquid fertilizer to half its recommended strength. Avoid contact with tender young fronds. Prune to remove all dead, broken fronds. Repot when roots become compacted. Propagate by division, runners.
Features: Good choice for hanging baskets, ledges, plant stands in bathrooms, kitchens, solariums. Mealybug, scale, spider mite susceptible.

Name: Fern, Northern Maidenhair. *Adiantum pedatum* fm. *imbricatum.* POLYPODIACEAE.

Description: Moderate-growing, upright, perennial, rhizomatous, evergreen fern, 1–2 ft. (30–60 cm) tall. Smooth, lacy, light green, branching fronds, to 1 ft. (30 cm) wide, with oval, finely cut leaflets, on wiry, black or purple leaf stalks.

Conditions: Light: indirect sun to partial shade. Humidity: 50–80%. Temperature: 45–60°F (7–16°C).

Soil: Well-drained, rich. 6.5–7.5 pH.

Care: Moderate. Water to keep soil evenly moist. Mist frequently. Fertilize monthly; dilute liquid fertilizer to half its recommended strength. Prune to remove all dead, broken fronds. Repot when roots become compacted. Propagate by division.

Features: Good choice for hanging baskets, ledges, plant stands in bathrooms, cool and low-light rooms. Scale susceptible.

Name: Fern, Shield; Holly Fern. *Polystichum* species. POLYPODIACEAE.

Description: About 120 species of moderate-growing, arching, perennial, rhizomatous, evergreen or sometimes deciduous ferns, to 4 ft. (1.2 m) tall outdoors, but indoors rarely over 2 ft. (60 cm). Leathery, spear-shaped, deep green, narrow, pointed fronds, to 4 ft. (1.2 m) long, with segmented, toothed leaflets, on fibrous-based leaf stalks. Grown for striking foliage. Korean rock fern, *P. tsus-simense,* is a commonly cultivated, small-stature species that tolerates low humidity.

Conditions: Light: filtered sun to partial shade. Humidity: 40–70%. Temperature: 50–70°F (10–21°C) spring–autumn, 45–60°F (7–16°C) winter.

Soil: Well-drained, rich. 6.5–7.0 pH.

Care: Easy. Water to keep soil evenly moist. Fertilize monthly; dilute liquid fertilizer to half its recommended strength. Prune to remove all dead, broken fronds. Repot when roots become compacted. Propagate by division, runners.

Features: Good choice for hanging baskets, ledges, plant stands in bathrooms, cool and low-light rooms. Pest and disease resistant.

Name: Fern, Squirrel's Foot. *Davallia trichomanoides.* POLYPODIACEAE.

Description: Moderate-growing, branching, perennial, rhizomatous, tropical, evergreen, epiphytic fern, to 1 ft. (30 cm) tall and 3 ft. (90 cm) wide. Feathery, green, spreading fronds, to 2 ft. (60 cm) long, on wiry leaf stalks. Brown, hairy-scaled rhizomes grow up and out of soil. Grown for foliage. Hare's foot fern, *D. canariensis,* with similar care needs and a more open appearance, is a closely related species.

Conditions: Light: indirect sun, 4–6 hours daily. Humidity: 50–80%. Temperature: 60–80°F (16–27°C).

Soil: Well-drained, sandy, rich–average. 5.5–6.5 pH.

Care: Easy. Water to keep soil evenly moist; reduce watering in winter. Mist occasionally. Fertilize monthly; dilute liquid fertilizer to half its recommended strength. Prune to remove all dead, broken fronds. Repot annually. Propagate by division, root layering.

Features: Good choice for hanging baskets, plant stands, tables, terrariums in bathrooms, kitchens, solariums. Mealybug, scale susceptible.

Name: Fig, Creeping; Creeping Rubber Plant. *Ficus pumila.* MORACEAE.

Description: Fast-growing, trailing, perennial, tropical, root-clinging vine, to 32 in. (80 cm) long or tall. Shiny, thin, deep green, heart-shaped or oval leaves, 2–4 in. (50–100 mm) long, on wiry leaf stems. Bears yellow, inedible figs. Grown primarily for foliage.

Conditions: Light: filtered sun to partial shade. Humidity: 50–80%. Temperature: 50–65°F (10–18°C).

Soil: Well-drained, rich. 6.0–7.0 pH.

Care: Moderate. Water to keep soil evenly moist. Mist frequently. Place in a stone-filled cachepot to add humidity. Fertilize bimonthly; dilute liquid fertilizer to half its recommended strength. Pinch to direct growth. Repot in spring when roots become compacted. Propagate by division, layering.

Features: Good choice for hanging baskets, sphagnum-filled poles, terrariums, topiary in cool, low-light rooms. Disease resistant. Spider mite susceptible.

Name: Fig, Fiddle-Leaf. *Ficus lyrata.* MORACEAE.

Description: Fast-growing, upright, tropical, deciduous tree, to 20 ft. (6 m) tall outdoors, but indoors rarely over 8 ft. (2.4 m). Leathery, shiny, paddle- or hourglass-shaped, deep green, wavy, veined leaves, to 16 in. (40 cm) long. Bears white-spotted, inedible figs. Grown for foliage. India rubber tree, *F. elastica,* is a commonly cultivated relative.

Conditions: Light: filtered sun, 2–4 hours daily. Humidity: 50–70%. Temperature: 60–75°F (16–24°C).

Soil: Well-drained, rich. 6.0–7.0 pH.

Care: Moderate. Water when soil surface dries. Mist occasionally. Fertilize monthly spring–autumn. Prune main growth buds to promote branching. Avoid sticky, staining sap. Repot semi-annually until plant reaches desired size; top dress thereafter. Propagate by stem layering.

Features: Good choice for floors, landings, in contemporary, tall-ceilinged rooms, entries. Mealybug, spider mite, scale susceptible.

Name: Fig, Weeping; Benjamin Tree. *Ficus benjamina.* MORACEAE.

Description: Medium- to slow-growing, upright, branching, open, tropical, deciduous tree, to 6 ft. (1.8 m) tall and nearly as wide. Shiny, thin, light green or variegated, oval leaves, 4 in. (10 cm) long, on attractive, sometimes hanging, gray-barked branches. Bears red, berrylike, inedible fruit. Grown for foliage. *F. benjamina* var. *nuda,* with narrow leaves, is a popular variety, as are the cultivars 'Hawaii', 'Starlight', and 'Gold Princess'.

Conditions: Light: filtered sun, 4–6 hours daily. Humidity: 40–70%. Temperature: 60–75°F (16–24°C). Sudden environmental change may cause complete leaf loss. Avoid overwatering; plant will sprout new leaves in 3–4 weeks.

Soil: Well-drained, rich. 6.0–7.0 pH.

Care: Easy. Water after soil dries. Fertilize bimonthly; dilute liquid fertilizer to half its recommended rate. Prune sparingly. Weave multiple trunks to create braided effects. Repot in spring when roots become compacted; top dress when mature. Propagate by stem layering.

Features: Good choice for espalier, floors, landings in bright rooms, entries, home offices. Mealybug, spider mite, scale susceptible.

Name: Flamingo Flower; Spathe Flower. *Anthurium* species. ARACEAE.

Description: More than 600 species and many hybrids of moderate-growing perennial, tropical, sometimes epiphytic herbs, 1–3 ft. (30–90 cm) tall. Textured, shiny or velvety, lance-shaped, deep green or sometimes bronze, pointed leaves, 8–16 in. (20–40 cm) long, on long stalks. Orange, pink, red, flat, waxy, heart-shaped, flowerlike bract supports an upright, yellow or orange, tail-shaped flower spike, or spathe. Spring–summer blooming. Only *A. scherzerianum* and *A.* × *andreanum* hybrids are commonly cultivated as houseplants.

Conditions: Light: filtered sun to full shade; requires bright indirect light in winter. Humidity: 60–90%. Temperature: 60–75°F (16–24°C).

Soil: Well-drained, rich. Plant epiphytic species in coarse bark. 6.0–7.0 pH.

Care: Moderate–challenging. Water to keep soil evenly moist; reduce watering in winter. Mist frequently. Mass several plants in a stone-filled cachepot to add humidity. Fertilize with each watering during growth; dilute liquid fertilizer to half its recommended rate. Deadhead spent flowers. Prune sparingly. Repot annually in spring. Propagate by stem cuttings, division, seed, suckers.

Features: Good choice for plant stands, tables, terrariums in low-light, warm rooms. Good for color, cutting, tropical flair. Aphid, spider mite susceptible.

Name: Fuchsia; Lady's-Eardrops. *Fuchsia* × *hybrida*. ONAGRACEAE.

Description: Many hybrids and cultivars of slow-growing, trailing, bushy, woody, evergreen shrubs, to 3 ft. (90 cm) tall and wide. Shiny, deep green or variegated, oval, pointed, slightly toothed leaves, to 2 in. (50 mm) long, in whorls around the stem. Bell-shaped, bicolored, red, orange, pink, purple, white, single, semi-double, double, or clustered, dangling flowers, to 3 in. (75 mm) long, with prominent stamens, on new wood. Summer blooming. Available in bush, trailing, or standard forms.

Conditions: Light: indirect sun, 4–6 hours daily; reduce light during winter. Humidity: 40–60%. Temperature: 50–75°F (10–24°C) during growth, 50–60°F (10–16°C) winter.

Soil: Well-drained, rich. 5.5–6.5 pH.

Care: Moderate. Water to keep soil evenly moist during growth; water sparingly in winter. Fertilize monthly during growth. Pinch growth tips to promote bushiness. Cut back severely in autumn to force dormancy and promote flowering. Repot annually in spring. Propagate by softwood cuttings.

Features: Good choice for hanging baskets, tables in cool rooms. Spider mite, whitefly, and brown spot susceptible.

Name: Geranium, Ivy. *Pelargonium peltatum*. GERANIACEAE.

Description: Many cultivars of fast-growing, climbing or trailing, perennial, fleshy herbs, to 3 ft. (90 cm) tall or long. Shiny, maplelike, green or sometimes red- or white-fringed, lobed leaves, to 3 in. (75 mm) wide, on trailing stems. Multiple, pink, red, white, star-shaped, single or double flowers, ½–2 in. (12–50 mm) wide, on long stalks. Summer–autumn blooming.

Conditions: Light: full sun, 4–6 hours daily. Humidity: 30–60%. Temperature: 50–70°F (10–21°C) during growth, 45–50°F (7–10°C) winter.

Soil: Well-drained, average. 7.0–7.5 pH.

Care: Easy. Water after soil dries; avoid wetting foliage. Fertilize monthly during growth with complete, low-nitrogen fertilizer. Deadhead spent flowers. Pinch growth tips to direct growth. Avoid repotting; produce new plants from cuttings. Propagate by stem cuttings, seed.

Features: Good choice for hanging baskets, ledges, plant stands, tables in bright, cool rooms. Aphid, spider mite and slug, snail susceptible.

Name: Geranium, Strawberry; Stawberry Begonia. *Saxifraga stolonifera.* SAXIFRAGACEAE.

Description: Several cultivars of fast-growing, mounding and trailing, fleshy, perennial herbs, to 9 in. (23 cm) tall and 1 ft. (30 cm) wide, with thin, hairy, strawberry-like runners bearing miniature plants, to 2 ft. (60 cm) long. Bristly or fuzzy, green or variegated, round, scalloped leaves, to 3 in. (75 mm) wide, with silver veins and reddish undersides. Multiple white flowers, to 1 in. (25 mm), with petals of varied lengths, form tall spikes. Summer blooming.

Conditions: Light: filtered sun, 3–5 hours daily. Humidity: 50–80%. Temperature: 50–60°F (10–16°C) during growth, 40–50°F (4–10°C) winter.

Soil: Well-drained, rich. 6.0–7.0 pH.

Care: Easy. Water to keep soil evenly moist during growth; water sparingly in winter. Mist occasionally. Fertilize monthly. Pinch growth tips to promote fullness. Repot annually in spring. Propagate by division, layering, runners.

Features: Good choice for hanging baskets, ledges, in cool, bright rooms. Pest and disease resistant.

Name: Geranium, Zonal; Bedding Geranium. *Pelargonium* x *hortorum.* GERANIACEAE.

Description: Many hybrids of fast-growing, mounding, bushy, perennial herbs, 2–4 ft. (60–120 cm) tall, with fleshy, brittle stems. Smooth, brown, green, or yellow, usually pink-banded, round, scalloped, and lobed leaves, to 5 in. (13 cm) wide. Clusters of orange, pink, purple, red, white, five-pointed flowers, 1–4 in. (25–100 mm) wide. Spring–summer blooming; some cultivars bloom year-round.

Conditions: Light: full sun, 3–5 hours daily. Humidity: 30–60%. Temperature: 55–70°F (13–21°C) during growth, 50–55°F (10–13°C) winter.

Soil: Well-drained, average. 7.0–7.5 pH.

Care: Easy. Water after soil dries; avoid wetting foliage. Fertilize monthly during growth with complete, low-nitrogen fertilizer. Deadhead spent flowers and leaves. Pinch growth tips to promote fullness. Repot when roots become crowded. Propagate by stem cuttings, seed.

Features: Good choice for hanging baskets, plant stands, windowsills in bright rooms, entries, halls. Mealybug, mildew, thrip susceptible.

Name: Gloxinia, Violet Slipper; Cinderella-Slippers. *Sinningia speciosa* grp. *maxima (S. regina).* GESNERIACEAE.

Description: Fast-growing, low and spreading, perennial, tropical tuber, to 1 ft. (30 cm) tall and wide. Textured, deep green, velvety, oval, scalloped leaves, to 6 in. (15 cm) long, with white veins above and purple beneath, in radiating clusters. Clusters of nodding, blue, orange, pink, purple, red, white, yellow, fringed, narrow, trumpet-shaped, often ruffled flowers, to 1 in. (25 mm) wide and 3 in. (75 mm) long. Summer–early autumn blooming. Florist's gloxinia, *S. speciosa* grp. *fyfiana*, with upturned flowers, is widely cultivated.

Conditions: Light: filtered or indirect sun, 4–6 hours daily. Humidity: 70–90%. Temperature: 60–70°F (16–21°C) during growth; store lifted tubers in dark in container of dry soil, 60°F (16°C).

Soil: Well-drained, rich. 6.0–6.5 pH.

Care: Easy. Water to keep evenly moist; avoid wetting foliage. Reduce watering after blooms fade, cease when leaves wither. Fertilize semi-monthly during growth. Store; repot in spring when new shoots emerge. Plant tuber 1 in. (25 mm) deep, hollow side up. Propagate by division, offsets, seed.

Features: Good choice for tables, windowsills in bright bathrooms, kitchens. Good for color, massed plantings. Aphid, thrip, and fungal disease susceptible.

Name: Goldfish Plant. *Columnea* species. GESNERIACEAE.

Description: More than 100 species and cultivars of slow-growing, mounded or trailing, perennial, succulent, epiphytic, brittle, evergreen vines or shrubs, to 3 ft. (90 cm) tall. Shiny or hairy, fleshy, deep green leaves, varied in length. Profuse orange, red, yellow, goldfish- or flute-shaped flowers, ½–1 in. (12–25 mm) long. Summer or year-round blooming, depending on species. Cultivars include 'Early Bird' and 'Mary Ann', with continuous blooms, and 'Aladdin's Lamp', with red blooms.

Conditions: Light: bright to filtered sun, 6–12 hours daily. Humidity: 60–85%. Temperature: 65–75°F (18–24°C).

Soil: Well-drained, loose bark chips or vermiculite-peat mix. 5.5–6.5 pH.

Care: Easy. Keep evenly moist. Fertilize semi-monthly during growth; dilute liquid fertilizer to half its recommended strength. Pinch growth tips to promote bushiness. Repot annually replacing bark chip mix. Propagate by cuttings, division, seed.

Features: Good choice for hanging baskets, ledges in bright rooms. Aphid, cyclamen mite, mealybug, leaf miner susceptible.

Name: Grape Ivy; Treebine. *Cissus rhombifolia.* VITACEAE.

Description: Fast-growing, climbing or trailing, dense, perennial, tropical, evergreen vine, to 6 ft. (1.8 m) tall, with hairy stems and long tendrils. Fuzzy becoming smooth, grapeleaflike, deep green, deeply lobed, scalloped leaves, 1–4 in. (25–100 mm) long. Flowers inconspicuous; grown primarily for foliage. Kangaroo vine, *C. antarctica,* with similar care needs, is commonly cultivated.

Conditions: Light: indirect sun, 4–6 hours daily. Humidity: 40–60%. Temperature: 60–70°F (16–21°C) spring–autumn, 45–55°F (7–13°C) winter.

Soil: Well-drained, average. 6.0–7.0 pH.

Care: Easy. Water only after soil dries. Mist occasionally. Fertilize quarterly spring–autumn. Pinch growth tips to direct growth. Prune bare stems above a leaf to renew growth. Repot annually in spring until plant reaches desired size; top dress annually thereafter with a layer of fresh soil, 1 in. (25 mm) thick. Propagate by cuttings, seed.

Features: Good choice for hanging baskets, sphagnum-filled poles in cool, dry, low-light rooms. Spider mite and fungal disease susceptible.

Name: Hen-and-Chickens; Mexican-Gem. *Echeveria elegans.* CRASSULACEAE.

Description: Slow-growing, flat and compact, perennial, succulent herb, to 3 in. (75 mm) high and 4 in. (10 cm) wide, with thick, short, strawberry-like, basal runners bearing miniature plants. Smooth, fleshy, brittle, petallike, silver gray to green and red-tinged, pointed leaves, 1½–2½ in. (38–65 mm) long, in rosettes. Clusters of pink, yellow, bell-shaped, nodding flowers, to ½ in. (12 mm) long, on medium spikes. Spring–summer blooming.

Conditions: Light: full sun, 6–8 hours daily. Humidity: 30–60%. Temperature: 50–80°F (10–27°C) spring–autumn, 45–60°F (7–16°C) winter.

Soil: Well-drained, sandy, average. 6.5–8.0 pH.

Care: Easy. Water only after soil completely dries; avoid wetting foliage. Fertilize monthly during growth; dilute liquid fertilizer to half its recommended rate. Turn frequently. Repot sparingly. Propagate by offsets.

Features: Good choice for low tables in bright rooms. Pest resistant. Fungal disease susceptible.

HERBS

Grow herbs right where you need them—in the kitchen. Besides adding pizzazz to meals, herbs make attractive houseplants. A variety of herbs grow well indoors. Most can be grown from seed, or you can buy rooted plants.

When choosing herb plants for indoor culture, look for those that are healthy with lots of bushy growth. Avoid rootbound plants. The smaller-leaved, more compact varieties usually make better indoor plants. Plant herbs separately. That way, if disease strikes one plant, you can quickly and easily remove it before the infection spreads to the others. Plant in well-draining organic potting soil in a site with good air circulation necessary to prevent leggy growth and avoid pests.

Place most herbs in a bright location, such as a western or eastern window. Plants will struggle near windows with too little light, and too sunny locations may become hot during midday, burning the herbs and causing dried or shriveled leaves. Herbs also do well under artificial light.

Pinch herbs regularly to keep them bushy, compact, and healthy. Always remove blooms from annual herbs, such as basil, because flowering will diminish leaf production and can change the flavor of the herb. Avoid pinching back perennial herbs more than halfway, as this can stunt their future growth. Ensure healthy growth by turning herbs once a week in the same direction so that all sides of the plant receive sun. Fertilize monthly with a balanced organic fertilizer. Replace weak or leggy plants once they become straggly with new, compact herbs.

In general, there are two categories of herbs—those that prefer a warm, sunny location, and those that require a little more shade and moister conditions. Here are the specific growing requirements for several popular kitchen herbs:

Sweet basil (*Ocimum basilicum*): This warm-season annual herb is best planted in the spring and summer months. It can be grown from seed or plants. Place this herb on a sunny windowsill or close to plant lights. Keep moist.

Chives (*Allium schoenoprasum*): A perennial that does well in a sunny window with rich, moist soil; it can be grown from seed or plants.

Mint (*Mentha* species): This perennial herb requires constant moisture and should be placed off to the side of the window as it grows better in filtered sunlight. Best if grown from cuttings.

Parsley (*Petroselinum crispum*): You can grow curly or flat-leafed Italian parsley. Provide it with moist soil and place it in filtered sunlight. This plant is technically a biennial but is generally grown as an annual from seed or plants. Speed seed germination before sowing by soaking in warm water 12 to 24 hours.

Rosemary (*Rosmarinus officinalis*): This long-lived perennial can survive indoors for many years if given the right conditions. The prostrate variety ('Prostratus') is your best choice. Give rosemary bright light and allow the soil to approach dryness before watering. Grow from plants or stem cuttings.

Sage (*Salvia officinalis*): There are many varieties of sage, which is a perennial. Place in bright light and allow the soil to approach dryness before watering. It can be grown from seed, plants, or cuttings.

Garden Thyme (*Thymus vulgaris*): There are many varieties of thyme. Your best choices are low-growing, trailing varieties. A perennial, this herb can be grown from seed, plants, or tip cuttings taken in spring. Place in bright light and allow soil to approach dryness before watering.

Chives

Garden thyme

(Left to right) Italian parsley, Dalmatian sage, rosemary, and English parsley.

Name: Hyacinth; Dutch Hyacinth; Garden Hyacinth. *Hyacinthus orientalis.* LILIACEAE.

Description: Many cultivars of erect, hardy, deciduous bulbs, to 1 ft. (30 cm) tall. Smooth, straplike, green, wavy-edged leaves, to 9 in. (23 cm) long. Multiple apricot, blue, orange, pink, purple, red, white, yellow, flared, trumpet-shaped, fragrant flowers, to 1 in. (25 mm) wide, in snug tiers vertically along the stalk, forming cone-shaped plumes. Spring blooming.

Conditions: Light: full to filtered sun, 4–6 hours daily. Humidity: 40–60%. Temperature: 50–60°F (10–16°C) during growth; store lifted bulbs in dark in net bag or open basket of dry peat moss, 40–50°F (4–10°C). After planting, chill 6–10 weeks at 35–45°F (2–7°C).

Soil: Well-drained, sandy, rich. 5.0–6.5 pH.

Care: Easy. Water to keep evenly moist during growth. Fertilize at planting. Deadhead after bloom and foliage withers; lift in late spring, store, and repot annually in autumn. Crowd plantings. Propagate by offsets.

Features: Good choice for windowsills in bright, cool rooms. Good for color, forcing, massed plantings. Pest and disease resistant.

Name: Ivy, Swedish; Swedish Begonia. *Plectranthus* species. LABIATAE.

Description: More than 250 species of fast-growing, trailing, dense, perennial, tropical herbs, to 3 ft. (90 cm) long. Fleshy, waxy, light green or variegated, oval, veined, finely toothed leaves, to 2½ in. (65 mm) long, often purple beneath. Clusters of blue, pink, white, mintlike flowers, on spikes, to 2 in. (50 mm) tall; grown primarily for striking foliage. Swedish ivy, *P. verticillatus (P. australis)*, and candle plant, *P. oertendahlii*, are commonly cultivated.

Conditions: Light: full to filtered sun, 5–7 hours daily. Humidity: 40–70%. Temperature: 60–75°F (16–24°C) spring–autumn, 50–60°F (10–16°C) winter.

Soil: Well-drained, rich–average. 6.5–7.5 pH.

Care: Easy. Water to keep soil evenly moist during growth; water sparingly in winter. Fertilize with each watering; dilute liquid fertilizer to half its recommended rate. Deadhead flower buds at formation. Pinch and prune frequently for dense foliage. Repot annually in spring. Propagate by cuttings, seed.

Features: Good choice for hanging baskets, ledges in bathrooms, home offices. Aphid, mealybug, whitefly susceptible.

Name: Lipstick Plant; Basket Plant. *Aeschynanthus lobbianus.* GESNERIACEAE.

Description: Fast-growing, trailing, perennial, hairy, tropical, epiphytic vine, to 18 in. (45 cm) long and 2 ft. (60 cm) wide. Leathery, deep green, oval, pointed leaves, to 2 in. (50 mm) long, on woody stems. Clusters of upturned, cream-throated, red, curved, tubular flowers, 2–3 in. (50–75 mm) long. Summer blooming. Several *Aeschynanthus* species with similar appearance and care requirements are cultivated, bearing orange, pink, yellow blooms.

Conditions: Light: indirect sun, 6–8 hours daily. Humidity: 50–80%. Temperature: 70–85°F (21–29°C) during growth, 55–65°F (13–18°C) winter.

Soil: Well-drained, average. 5.5–6.5 pH.

Care: Modereate–challenging. Water to keep soil evenly moist during growth; reduce watering in winter. Fertilize with each watering. Prune away longest stems after flowering. Repot in spring when crowded. Propagate by stem cuttings, division, seed.

Features: Good choice for hanging baskets, ledges in bright, warm rooms, solariums. Aphid, mealybug, thrip susceptible.

Name: Mosaic Plant; Nerve Plant. *Fittonia verschaffeltii.* ACANTHACEAE.
Description: Fast-growing, trailing or creeping, hairy, perennial, tropical herb, to 3 in. (75 mm) high and 18 in. (45 cm) wide. Textured, mintlike, olive green, white- or red-veined, pointed, toothed leaves, to 4 in. (10 cm) long. Flowers insignificant; grown primarily for foliage. A related species, *F. gigantea,* bearing dark green leaves with bright red veins, grows 18 in. (45 cm) tall. Dwarf cultivars available.
Conditions: Light: partial shade. Humidity: 70–90%. Temperature: 60–70°F (16–21°C). Maintain steady temperature and humidity.
Soil: Well-drained, rich. 6.0–7.0 pH.
Care: Moderate. Water to keep soil evenly moist. Mist frequently. Mass several plants in a stone-filled cachepot to add humidity. Fertilize with each watering; dilute acidic liquid fertilizer to half its recommended rate. Pinch frequently for dense foliage. Repot annually in spring. Propagate by stem cuttings, division.
Features: Good choice for hanging baskets, terrariums in bathrooms, low-light rooms. Good ground cover. Pest and disease resistant.

Name: Narcissus; Daffodil; Jonquil. *Narcissus* species. AMARYLLIDACEAE.
Description: About 50 species and thousands of cultivars of erect, hardy, deciduous bulbous herbs, 4–24 in. (10–60 cm) tall. Narrow, light to dark green, flat, straplike leaves, to 1 ft. (30 cm) long. Single or clustered, cream, orange, peach, pink, red, white, yellow, bicolored, trumpet-shaped, sometimes fragrant flowers, ½–2 in. (12–50 mm) wide, with short to long, smooth or ruffled crowns. Spring blooming.
Conditions: Light: full to filtered sun, 6–8 hours daily. Humidity: 40–70%. Temperature: 45–60°F (7–16°C) during growth; store lifted bulbs in dark in net bag or open basket of dry peat moss, 40–50°F (4–10°C). After planting, chill 10–12 weeks at 35–45°F (2–7°C).
Soil: Well-drained, rich. 5.5–6.5 pH.
Care: Easy. Water to keep soil evenly moist; withhold water for 4–6 weeks in late spring to force dormancy. Fertilize only at planting. Stake to support flower stalks. Deadhead after bloom and foliage withers; lift in late spring, store, and repot annually in autumn. Crowd plantings. Propagate by offsets.
Features: Good choice for windowsills in bright, cool kitchens, bathrooms. Good for color, forcing, massed plantings. Disease resistant. Narcissus bulb fly succeptible.

Name: Orange Jasmine; Orange Jessamine. *Murraya paniculata (M. exotica).* RUTACEAE.
Description: Slow-growing, branching, open, evergreen, woody, tropical shrub, to over 15 ft. (4.6 m) tall outdoors, but indoors rarely over 6 ft. (1.8 m). Shiny, deep green, 3–9-leaflet, nodding, oval leaves, to 3 in. (75 mm) long. Single, white, fragrant flowers, to ½ in. (12 mm) long, develop red, berrylike fruits. Intermittent, year-round blooming. Dwarf cultivars available. Leaves of a related species, *M. koenigii,* is the source of curry spice.
Conditions: Light: filtered or indirect sun, 4–6 hours daily. Humidity: 30–70%. Temperature: 70–80°F (21–27°C).
Soil: Well-drained, rich. 6.0–7.5 pH.
Care: Easy–moderate. Water when soil surface dries. Fertilize monthly spring–autumn. Prune sparingly. Repot annually until mature; top dress annually thereafter. Propagate by layering, seed.
Features: Good choice for floors, landings in bright rooms, entries, home offices, solariums. Pest and disease resistant.

Name: Orchid Pansy; Cupid's-Bower. *Achimenes* species. GESNERIACEAE.

Description: More than 25 species of deciduous, mounding, perennial, rhizomatous, tropical herbs, 1–2 ft. (30–60 cm) tall. Textured, hairy, olive green, oval, finely toothed leaves, to 3½ in. (90 mm) long. Multiple, blue, orange, pink, purple, red, yellow, white, flutelike flowers, 1–2 in. (25–50 mm) long, with thin or broad, flared petals and white throats. Summer–autumn blooming. Cupid's-bower, *A. grandiflora*, is commonly cultivated in specialty nurseries.

Conditions: Light: full or filtered sun, 5–8 hours daily. Humidity: 60–80%. Temperature: 60–80°F (16–27°C) during growth; store lifted rhizome in dark in porous container of dampened peat moss, 50–60°F (10–16°C).

Soil: Well-drained, rich. 6.0–7.0 pH.

Care: Easy. Water to keep soil evenly moist during growth; withhold water for 4–6 weeks in late summer to force dormancy. Fertilize with each watering until bloom; dilute liquid fertilizer to quarter its recommended rate. Deadhead after blooms, foliage withers; lift in autumn, store, and repot in spring. Propagate by division.

Features: Good choice for ledges in bright, warm rooms. Good for color. Spider mite, thrip susceptible.

Name: Orchid, Cymbidium. *Cymbidium* species. ORCHIDACEAE.

Description: More than 40 species and many hybrids of slow-growing, upright, spreading, perennial, epiphytic plants, to 3 ft. (90 cm) tall. Leathery, shiny, straplike, green, narrow, pointed leaves, to 18 in. (45 cm) long, form sheaths around a bulblike base with green air roots. Multiple, waxy, brown, cream, green, pink, purple, red, white, yellow, sometimes variegated, striped or spotted, 5-petaled flowers, to 3 in. (75 mm) wide, with distinctive central pedestals, in tiers vertically along the stalk. Winter–spring blooming.

Conditions: Light: indirect sun, 4–6 hours daily. Humidity: 50–70%. Temperature: 65–85°F (18–29°C) during growth; nighttime temperature of 45–55°F (7–13°C) needed to form buds.

Soil: Well-drained, loose bark chips. 5.5–6.5 pH.

Care: Moderate. Water to keep bark evenly moist during growth; reduce watering in winter. Fertilize with each watering; dilute acidic liquid fertilizer to half its recommended strength. Stake flower stalks. Deadhead spent flowers. Prune sparingly. Repot annually; replace all bark. Propagate by division.

Features: Good choice for hanging baskets, ledges, tables, windowsills in bright rooms. Good for cutting. Fungal disease susceptible.

Name: Orchid, Moth. *Phalaenopsis* species. ORCHIDACEAE.

Description: More than 55 species of slow-growing, upright, spreading, tropical, perennial, sometimes epiphytic herbs, to 18 in. (45 cm) tall. Smooth, fleshy or leathery, green, wide, pointed leaves, to 1 ft. (30 cm) long, rise from basal stalks with gray air roots. Multiple, velvety, pink, purple, red, white, yellow, often spotted flowers, to 2–5 in. (50–125 mm) wide, with wing-shaped petals and contrasting base pedestals, in tiers on arching stalks. Spring–autumn blooming.

Conditions: Light: indirect sun, 4–6 hours daily. Humidity: 60–80%. Temperature: 70–85°F (21–29°C) days, 60–70°F (16–21°C) nights.

Soil: Well-drained, loose bark chips or slab with sphagnum moss. 5.5–6.5 pH.

Care: Easy–moderate. Water after bark dries. Mass several plants in a stone-filled cachepot to add humidity. Fertilize with each watering; dilute acidic liquid fertilizer to half its recommended strength. Stake flower stalks. Repot semi-annually; replace all bark. Propagate by division.

Features: Good choice for bark slabs, hanging baskets, tables, windowsills in bright rooms. Fungal disease susceptible.

Name: Palm, Clustered Fishtail. *Caryota mitis.* PALMAE.

Description: Slow-growing, upright, clustering, tropical palm, to 40 ft. (12 m) tall outdoors, but indoors rarely over 10 ft. (3 m). Unique, smooth, fishtaillike, light green, rectangular, veined leaves, to 6 in. (15 cm) long and 4 in. (10 cm) wide, with ragged-toothed leaflets. Flowers are white, datelike clusters, on woody basal stems, forming fleshy seeds; grown primarily for foliage. Related species are taller, to 100 ft. (30.5 m).

Conditions: Light: filtered or indirect sun, 5–8 hours daily. Humidity: 30–70%. Temperature: 60–80°F (16–27°C) spring–autumn, 50–60°F (10–16°C) winter.

Soil: Well-drained, rich. 6.0–7.0 pH.

Care: Moderate. Water to keep soil evenly moist during growth; reduce watering in winter. Mist and wipe foliage occasionally. Fertilize monthly. Deadhead spent fronds. Pinch emerging flower spikes. Repot when crowded. Propagate by division, offsets.

Features: Good choice for floors, landings in bathrooms, halls, home offices, solariums. Good for tropical flair. Scale, spider mite and fungal disease susceptible.

Name: Palm, Miniature Date; Pygmy Date Palm. *Phoenix roebelenii.* PALMAE.

Description: Slow-growing, spreading, clustering, tropical palm, to 20 ft. (6 m) tall outdoors, but indoors rarely over 10 ft. (3 m). Shiny, arching, deep green, broad fronds, to 4 ft. (1.2 m) long, divided into more than 100 fine, grass- or willowlike pinnae, each to 10 in. (25 cm) long. White clustered flowers, on a stalk to 18 in. (45 cm) long, develop black, berrylike fruit; grown primarily for foliage.

Conditions: Light: filtered or indirect sun, 5–8 hours daily. Humidity: 25–60%. Temperature: 60–80°F (16–27°C) spring–autumn, 50–60°F (10–16°C) winter.

Soil: Well-drained, rich. 6.0–7.0 pH.

Care: Easy–moderate. Water when soil surface dries; reduce watering in winter. Mist and wipe foliage occasionally. Fertilize monthly. Deadhead spent fronds. Pinch emerging flower spikes. Prune suckers to maintain single trunk. Repot when crowded. Propagate by division, offsets.

Features: Good choice for floors, landings in bathrooms, halls, home offices, solariums. Good for tropical effects. Mostly pest and disease resistant. Scale, nematode, spider mite and fungal disease susceptible.

Name: Palm, Parlor; Feather Palm; Good-Luck Palm. *Chamaedorea elegans (Neanthe bella).* PALMAE.

Description: Slow-growing, upright or bushy, caning, tropical palm, to 4 ft. (1.2 m) tall. Shiny, arching, deep green, broad fronds, to 3 ft. (90 cm) long, divided into 40–80 narrow pinnae, each to 8 in. (20 cm) long. Flowers insignificant; grown primarily for foliage.

Conditions: Light: partial shade. Humidity: 40–80%. Temperature: 60–80°F (16–27°C) spring–autumn, 50–60°F (10–16°C) winter.

Soil: Well-drained, average. 5.5–6.5 pH.

Care: Easy. Water only after soil dries. Fertilize monthly. Deadhead spent fronds. Repot when crowded. Propagate by division.

Features: Good choice for floors, landings, tables in bathrooms, halls, home offices, low-light rooms. Good for tropical effects. Drought tolerant. Scale, nematode, spider mite susceptible.

Name: Papyrus, Dwarf; Miniature Papyrus. *Cyperus prolifer (C. isocladus).* CYPERACEAE.
Description: Fast-growing, upright, grasslike, perennial, rhizomatous sedge, to 18 in. (45 cm) tall, with brittle, triangular-shaped stems in cross section. Smooth, radiating, grasslike blue green, basal leaves and umbrella-like, clustered rays atop stems form distinctive foliage. Multiple, brown, grasslike, clustered flowers mingle between rays and develop lens-shaped seeds. Grown for foliage.
Conditions: Light: filtered sun, 6–8 hours daily. Humidity: 60–80%. Temperature: 60–80°F (16–27°C).
Soil: Well-drained, moist, rich. 5.5–7.0 pH.
Care: Easy. Water to keep soil evenly moist, using dechlorinated water. Fertilize quarterly. Deadhead spent stalks. Prune to growth point to renew. Repot annually in spring. Propagate by division, seed.
Features: Good choice for tables in bathrooms, bright rooms, modern interiors. Good for contemporary flair. Mass in submerged saucer to create indoor bogs. Pest and disease resistant.

Name: Peace Lily; White Flag; White Sail. *Spathiphyllum wallisii.* ARACEAE.
Description: Moderate-growing, spreading, perennial, rhizomatous, tropical herb, to 16 in. (40 cm) tall. Shiny, lance-shaped, deep green, broad, wavy, pointed leaves, to 6 in. (15 cm) long, on clustered, woody leaf stalks. Cream, white, hoodlike, flowerlike bract, to 3 in. (75 mm) long, surrounds an upright, yellow or white, tail-shaped flower spike, or spathe, forming an arum- or callalike flower on a tall stalk. Spring–autumn blooming.
Conditions: Light: indirect sun to partial shade. Humidity: 40–60%. Temperature: 60–80°F (16–27°C).
Soil: Well-drained, rich. 5.5–7.0 pH.
Care: Easy. Water when soil surface dries. Mist and wipe foliage occasionally. Fertilize with each watering; dilute acidic liquid fertilizer to half its recommended rate. Deadhead spent flower stalks. Repot semi-annually in spring. Propagate by division.
Features: Good choice for hanging baskets, ledges, plant stands, tables in bathrooms, bedrooms, low-light rooms. Mealybug, spider mite, and fungal disease susceptible.

Name: Philodendron, Heart-Leaf; Parlor Ivy. *Philodendron scandens.* ARACEAE.
Description: Several subspecies of fast-growing, trailing or vining, evergreen, epiphytic herbs, to 50 ft. (15 m) long outdoors, but indoors rarely over 15 ft. (4.6 m), with white, brown air roots along vinelike stems. Shiny, heart-shaped, deep green, sometimes russet, solid, veined, pointed leaves, to 1 ft. (30 cm) long. Flowers rare; grown primarily for foliage.
Conditions: Light: indirect sun to partial shade. Humidity: 40–70%. Temperature: 50–75°F (10–24°C).
Soil: Well-drained, rich. 5.5–6.5 pH.
Care: Easy. Water to keep soil evenly moist; reduce watering in winter. Fertilize with each watering; dilute acidic liquid fertilizer to half its recommended strength. Avoid wetting foliage. Deadhead spent leaves. Stake on fibrous pole to support upright vines or allow to trail. Pinch growth tips to promote fullness. Prune to renew. Repot when crowded. Propagate by stem cuttings, layering in summer.
Features: Good choice for hanging baskets, floors, landings, ledges in low-light, cool rooms. Aphid, mealybug and fungal disease susceptible.

Name: Pickaback Plant; Piggyback Plant; Mother-of-Thousands. *Tolmiea menziesii.* SAXIFRAGACEAE.

Description: Fast-growing, mounding or trailing, perennial, rhizomatous herb, to 1 ft. (30 cm) tall. Textured, hairy, heart-shaped, light green or variegated, lobed and toothed, veined, pointed leaves, to 4 in. (10 cm) wide, on dangling stems. Flowers rare; grown primarily for foliage.

Conditions: Light: filtered sun to partial shade. Humidity: 40–70%. Temperature: 45–60°F (7–16°C).

Soil: Well-drained, rich–average. 6.0–7.0 pH.

Care: Easy. Water to keep soil evenly moist; reduce watering in winter. Fertilize monthly during growth. Pinch growth tips to control growth. Repot annually in spring until plant becomes leggy; propagate and discard. Propagate by division, layering of plantlets formed on upper surface of mature leaves.

Features: Good choice for hanging baskets, ledges, plant stands, tables in cool rooms, halls. Disease resistant. Mealybug, spider mite, whitefly susceptible.

Name: Pineapple. *Ananas* species. BROMELIACEAE.

Description: About 9 species of slow-growing, radiating, perennial, tropical herbs, to 3 ft. (90 cm) tall. Shiny, fleshy, spear-shaped, green, red, white, striped or variegated, arching leaves, to 2 ft. (60 cm) long, scalloped and armed with sharp spines. Striking, pink, red, stalked flowers on 4–6-year-old plants form fragrant, inedible, pineapple-like fruits. *A. nanus* is a dwarf cultivar. Edible pineapple, *A. comosus*, with solid green leaves, becomes too large for houseplant use.

Conditions: Light: full sun, 6–8 hours daily. Humidity: 60–80%. Temperature: 50–85°F (10–29°C); sustained temperatures over 80°F (27°C) needed to form flowers.

Soil: Well-drained, rich. 6.0–7.0 pH.

Care: Moderate. Apply demineralized water to central cup of plant. Mist frequently. Fertilize semi-monthly with watering; dilute foliar fertilizer to half its recommended rate. Repot annually in spring. Propagate by offsets.

Features: Good choice for floors, tables, windowsills in bright, warm rooms. Good for children, contemporary flair. Cut tops of edible pineapple will root in warm, moist potting soil. Pest and disease resistant.

Name: Polka-Dot Plant; Flamingo Plant; Freckle-Face. *Hypoestes phyllostachya (H. sanguinolenta).* ACANTHACEAE.

Description: Fast-growing, mounding, dense, perennial, evergreen herb, to 2 ft. (60 cm) tall. Smooth, deep green, pink, white, spotted or variegated, oval, veined, pointed leaves, to 2½ in. (65 mm) long. Flowers inconspicuous; grown primarily for foliage.

Conditions: Light: full to filtered sun, 4–6 hours daily. Humidity: 40–60%. Temperature: 60–75°F (16–24°C).

Soil: Well-drained, rich–average. 6.0–7.0 pH.

Care: Easy. Water to keep soil evenly moist; reduce watering in winter. Fertilize monthly. Pinch to control growth; prune foliage, roots to maintain size, renew. Repot annually in spring. Propagate by stem cuttings, seed.

Features: Good choice for hanging baskets, ledges, terrariums in bright rooms. Good for color. Mealybug, scale, spider mite, whitefly susceptible.

Name: Ponytail Palm; Elephant-Foot Tree. *Nolina recurvata* var. *intermedia (Beaucarnea recurvata).* AGAVACEAE.

Description: Very slow growing, erect, branching, palm- or treelike plant, to 15 ft. (4.6 m) tall outdoors, but indoors rarely over 6 ft. (1.8 m), with pronounced, swollen trunk base. Shiny, straplike, deep green, narrow, wavy, pointed leaves, to 5 ft. (1.5 m) long, form a globular, plumelike crown. Flowers rare; grown primarily for structural form.

Conditions: Light: full to filtered sun, 4–8 hours daily. Humidity: 10–50%. Temperature: 50–100°F (10–38°C).

Soil: Well-drained, sandy, average. 7.0–8.0 pH.

Care: Easy. Water only after soil completely dries. Fertilize quarterly spring–autumn. Tolerant of intermittent care. Avoid pruning. Repot only when roots emerge from pot. Propagate by offsets, seed.

Features: Good choice for floors, landings, windows in bright, hot rooms. Good for southwestern regional flair. Pest resistant. Fungal disease susceptible.

Name: Pothos; Devil's Ivy; Hunter's-Robe; Philodendron. *Epipremnum aureum (Scindapsus aureus).* ARACEAE.

Description: Fast-growing, climbing or vining, tropical, evergreen herb, to 40 ft. (12 m) long outdoors, but indoors rarely over 8 ft. (2.4 m). Shiny, heart-shaped, green, white, yellow-variegated, veined, pointed leaves, to 1 ft. (30 cm) long. Flowers rare; grown primarily for foliage. A related species, *E. pinnatum,* is similar in form and climbs to great height.

Conditions: Light: indirect sun, 4–6 hours daily. Humidity: 50–80%. Temperature: 50–80°F (10–27°C).

Soil: Well-drained, rich. 5.5–6.5 pH.

Care: Easy. Water when soil surface dries. Fertilize with each watering; dilute acidic liquid fertilizer to half its recommended strength. Deadhead spent leaves. Stake on fibrous pole to support upright vines or allow to trail. Pinch growth tips to promote fullness. Prune to renew. Repot when crowded. Propagate by stem cuttings, layering in spring–summer.

Features: Good choice for hanging baskets, floors, landings, ledges, walls in bathrooms, kitchens. Aphid, mealybug, and fungal disease susceptible.

Name: Prayer Plant. *Maranta leuconeura.* MARANTACEAE.

Description: Slow-growing, branching or spreading, dense, perennial, tropical, evergreen herb, to 1 ft (30 cm) tall and 18 in. (45 cm) wide. Satin-textured, light–deep green, variegated, oval, pointed leaves, to 6 in. (15 cm) long, with veins of red, white, or yellow. Flowers insignificant; grown for distinctive foliage. Closely related to *Calathea, Ctenanthe,* and *Stromanthe.*

Conditions: Light: indirect sun to partial shade. Humidity: 60–80%. Temperature: 60–75°F (16–24°C).

Soil: Well-drained, rich. 6.0–7.0 pH.

Care: Easy. Water to keep soil evenly moist; reduce watering in winter. Use distilled or dechlorinated water. Fertilize with each watering; dilute liquid fertilizer to half its recommended strength. Protect from direct sun. Pinch growth points to direct growth. Repot semi-annually in spring. Propagate by crown division, stem cuttings.

Features: Good choice for hanging baskets, columns, ledges in cool rooms, bathrooms. Good for color. Leaves fold and close at night. Mealybug, spider mite susceptible.

Name: Radiator Plant; Emerald-Ripple Peperomia. *Peperomia caperata*, *P. caperata* var. *variegata*. PIPERACEAE.

Description: Slow-growing, compact and mounding, perennial, succulent, tropical, evergreen herb, 6–8 in. (15–20 cm) tall. Deeply textured, fleshy, heart-shaped, deep green, veined, pointed leaves, to 2 in. (50 mm) long, on pink or red leaf stalks. Spikelike, white, narrow flower stalks, to 4 in. (10 cm) tall. Year-round blooming; grown primarily for foliage. 'Little Fantasy', with white-edged leaves, is commonly cultivated.

Conditions: Light: indirect sun to partial shade. Humidity: 50–80% during growth; 40–60% winter. Temperature: 50–75°F (10–24°C).

Soil: Well-drained, rich–average. 6.0–7.0 pH.

Care: Easy. Water only after soil dries. Fertilize monthly spring–autumn; dilute liquid fertilizer to half its recommended strength. Pinch growth tips to control growth. Avoid repotting. Propagate by leaf, stem cuttings in summer.

Features: Good choice for terrariums in bathrooms, kitchens, low-light rooms. Good for mixed plantings. Pest and disease resistant.

Name: Rosary Vine; Hearts-on-a-String. *Ceropegia woodii*. ASCLEPIADACEAE.

Description: Slow-growing, trailing, sparse, tropical, evergreen, tuberous vine, to 3 ft. (90 cm) long. Pairs of waxy, heart-shaped, silver gray, succulent, pointed leaves, to 1 in. (25 mm) long, with purple undersides, dangle on brittle, wirelike stems. Insignificant flowers; grown for foliage.

Conditions: Light: full to filtered sun, 4–6 hours daily. Humidity: 20–40%. Temperature: 50–75°F (10–24°C).

Soil: Well-drained, sandy, average. 6.5–7.5 pH.

Care: Easy. Water when soil surface dries; water sparingly in winter. Fertilize monthly spring–autumn. Prune longest strands to renew. Repot in spring. Propagate by cuttings in spring–summer.

Features: Good choice for hanging baskets, columns, ledges in bright bedrooms, halls, sitting rooms, solariums. Good for mixed plantings. Pest and disease resistant.

Name: Sensitive Plant. *Mimosa pudica*. LEGUMINOSAE.

Description: Slow-growing, branching, bushy, woody, spiny, tropical, evergreen shrub, to 3 ft. (90 cm) tall. Smooth, fernlike, green, feathery leaves, to 5 in. (13 cm) long, divided into 15–25 pairs of narrow, touch-sensitive leaflets, to 1 in. (25 mm) long, close when brushed. Fluffy, pink, globular flowers, to ½ in. (12 mm) long. Summer blooming.

Conditions: Light: full to filtered sun, 4–6 hours daily. Humidity: 60–80%. Temperature: 60–80°F (16–27°C).

Soil: Well-drained, average. 6.0–7.5 pH.

Care: Moderate. Water to keep soil evenly moist; reduce watering in winter. Fertilize quarterly spring–autumn. Prune to shape. Avoid repotting. Propagate by stem cuttings in spring–summer, seed; soak seed in hot water before sowing.

Features: Good choice for terrariums in bright, warm rooms. Good for children to explore and learn about how plants react to their environment. Leaves reopen 30–45 minutes after being touched. Pest and disease resistant.

Name: Shrimp Plant. *Justicia brandegeana (Beloperone guttata)*. ACANTHACEAE.
Description: Moderate-growing, mounding, open, tropical, perennial, evergreen shrub, to 3 ft. (90 cm) tall. Textured, soft, hairy, tear-shaped, deep green, oval, pointed leaves, to 3 in. (75 mm) long, on weak leaf stalks. Tight prawnlike spikes of tube-shaped, nodding, purple, red, white flowers, with green, orange, pink, salmon, yellow segmented bracts, to 6 in. (15 cm) long. Spring–autumn blooming.
Conditions: Light: full to filtered sun, 3–4 hours daily. Humidity: 30–60%. Temperature: 60–80°F (16–27°C) during growth, 50–60°F (10–16°C) winter.
Soil: Well-drained, rich–average. 6.5–7.5 pH.
Care: Easy. Water when soil surface dries; reduce watering in winter. Fertilize monthly during growth. Deadhead spent blooms. Pinch to remove early buds. Prune to half size in spring. Repot only when crowded in spring. Propagate by stem cuttings, seed.
Features: Good choice for hanging baskets, plant stands, tables, terrariums, windowsills in bright, warm rooms. Good for color. Pest and disease resistant.

Name: Snake Plant; Mother-in-Law's Tongue. *Sansevieria trifasciata*. AGAVACEAE.
Description: Slow-growing, upright, spreading, perennial, succulent, rhizomatous, evergreen herb, to 3 ft. (90 cm) tall. Shiny, fleshy, sword-shaped, green banded and marbled, arching, pointed leaves, to 4 ft. (1.2 m) long, armed with a sharp terminal spine. Fragrant, cream white flower spikes rare; grown primarily for foliage. *S. trifasciata* 'Laurentii', with golden edges, is commonly cultivated.
Conditions: Light: filtered sun to shade. Humidity: 20–50%. Temperature: 60–80°F (16–27°C) spring–autumn, 50–60°F (10–16°C) winter.
Soil: Well-drained, sandy, rich. 6.5–8.0 pH.
Care: Easy. Water only after soil dries; avoid wetting foliage. Reduce watering in winter. Fertilize monthly; dilute liquid fertilizer to half its recommended rate. Tolerant of intermittent care. Avoid repotting. Propagate by division, offsets; rooted leaf cuttings lack distinctive coloration.
Features: Good choice for bright or low-light rooms, home offices. Good for contemporary flair. Mostly pest and disease resistant. Mealybug susceptible.

Name: Spider Plant; Spider Ivy. *Chlorophytum comosum (C. capense)*. LILIACEAE.
Description: Fast-growing, trailing, open, perennial, rhizomatous herb, to 3 ft. (90 cm) tall, with strawberry-like runners bearing miniature plants. Shiny, leathery, sword-shaped, green-, white-, yellow-banded, arching, pointed leaves, to 18 in. (45 cm) long, in rosettes. Insignificant, white, clustered flowers rare; grown primarily for foliage. Dwarf cultivars available.
Conditions: Light: indirect sunlight, 4–6 hours daily. Humidity: 30–60%. Temperature: 60–75°F (16–24°C) spring–autumn, 45–60°F (7–16°C) winter.
Soil: Well-drained, average. 6.0–7.5 pH.
Care: Easy. Water when soil surface dries; reduce watering in winter. When roots become compacted, water by pot submersion. Mist occasionally. Fertilize monthly; dilute liquid fertilizer to half its recommended rate. Trim off brown leaf ends. Repot when roots become compacted in spring. Propagate by division, plantlets.
Features: Good choice for hanging baskets, ledges, plant stands, window-sills in bedrooms, entries, halls, home offices. Aphid, scale susceptible.

Name: Split-Leaf Philodendron; Mexican Breadfruit; Swiss-Cheese Plant. *Monstera deliciosa.* ARACEAE.

Description: Fast-growing, climbing or vining, tropical, evergreen, epiphytic herb, to 30 ft. (9 m) long, with brown air roots along vinelike stems. Shiny, heart-shaped, deep green or variegated, veined, pointed leaves, to 1 ft. (30 cm) long, often cut or perforated to midrib. Mature plants bear callalike, yellow, spiked flowers enclosed in white bracts, in summer, developing edible, banana-flavored fruits; grown primarily for foliage.

Conditions: Light: filtered or indirect sun, 4–6 hours daily. Humidity: 40–70%. Temperature: 65–85°F (18–29°C) spring–autumn, 50–70°F (10–21°C) winter.

Soil: Well-drained, rich. 5.5–6.5 pH.

Care: Easy. Water when soil surface dries; reduce watering in winter. Fertilize with each watering; dilute acidic liquid fertilizer to half its recommended strength. Avoid wetting foliage. Deadhead spent leaves. Stake on fibrous pole to support upright vines or allow to trail. Pinch growth tips to promote fullness. Prune to renew. Repot when crowded. Propagate by cuttings of growth tip with air root, layering in summer.

Features: Good choice for floors, landings, ledges in sitting rooms, tall-ceilinged rooms. Provide more light to increase leaf splits. Aphid, scale, spider mite, and fungal disease susceptible.

Name: String-of-Beads. *Senecio rowleyanus.* ASTERACEAE (COMPOSITAE).

Description: Slow-growing, matting or trailing, perennial, succulent herb, to 16 in. (40 cm) long. Unusual, smooth, pearl-like, green, banded, spherical leaves, to ¼ in. (6 mm) in diameter, dangle vertically on wirelike stems. Lacks flowers; grown for unique foliage. Related species *S. herreianus*, with oval beads, and *S. citriformis*, with lemon-shaped beads, require similar care.

Conditions: Light: filtered sun, 4–6 hours daily. Humidity: 40–60%. Temperature: 60–80°F (16–27°C) spring–autumn, 50–70°F (10–21°C) winter.

Soil: Well-drained, average. 6.5–7.5 pH.

Care: Easy. Water after soil completely dries. Fertilize monthly. Tolerant of intermittent care. Deadhead withered stems. Repot when crowded in spring. Propagate by stem layering.

Features: Good choice for hanging baskets, ledges in bedrooms, entries, bright rooms. Good for children. Aphid, spider mite susceptible.

Name: Ti; Good-Luck Plant; Tree-of-Kings. *Cordyline terminalis.* AGAVACEAE.

Description: Moderate-growing, mounding or upright, perennial, fibrous-rooted, tropical, false palm, to 10 ft. (3 m) tall outdoors, but indoors rarely over 6 ft. (1.8 m). Shiny, sword-shaped, solid green or cream, pink-, purple-, red-variegated, narrow, pointed leaves, to 1 ft. (30 cm) long. Creamy flowers rare; grown for foliage. Several related species are woody, treelike plants with swordlike leaves, resembling yucca and agave. Sometimes confused with *Dracaena* species.

Conditions: Light: full or indirect sun, 3–4 hours daily. Humidity: 50–70%. Temperature: 60–75°F (16–24°C).

Soil: Well-drained, sandy, average. 6.5–7.5 pH.

Care: Easy. Water to keep soil evenly moist. Fertilize monthly. Mist occasionally. Trim brown leaf tips with scissors. Repot if crowded. Propagate by stem cuttings, layering.

Features: Good choice for floors, landings in solariums, low-light and tall-ceilinged rooms. Good for tropical effects. Pest and disease resistant.

Name: Tulip. *Tulipa* species. LILIACEAE.

Description: About 100 species and thousands of cultivars of erect, hardy, deciduous, tunicate, bulbous herbs, 5–24 in. (13–60 cm) tall. Narrow to broad, light to dark green, flat, straplike or tear-shaped leaves, to 1 ft. (30 cm) long. Solitary, in all colors except blue, and bi-, multicolored, egg-shaped, sometimes fragrant flowers, to 4 in. (10 cm) wide, with single or double, rounded or pointed, smooth or fringed petals. Spring blooming.

Conditions: Light: full to filtered sun, 6–8 hours daily. Humidity: 40–70%. Temperature: 45–60°F (7–16°C) during growth; store lifted bulbs in dark in net bag or open basket of dry peat moss, 40–50°F (4–10°C). After planting, chill 15–18 weeks at 35–45°F (2–7°C).

Soil: Well-drained, rich–average. 5.5–6.5 pH.

Care: Easy. Water to keep soil evenly moist; withhold water for 4–6 weeks after blooms fade to force dormancy. Fertilize only at planting. Stake to support flower stalks. Deadhead after bloom and foliage withers; lift in late spring, store, and repot annually in autumn. Crowd plantings. Propagate by offsets.

Features: Good choice for tables, windowsills in bright, cool rooms. Good for color, forcing, massed plantings. Disease resistant. Aphid succeptible.

Name: Umbrella Tree; Octopus Tree; Rubber Tree; Starleaf. *Schefflera actinophylla (Brassaia actinophylla)*. ARALIACEAE.

Description: Fast-growing, branching, upright, tropical, evergreen, treelike shrub, to 40 ft. (12 m) outdoors, but indoors rarely over 15 ft. (4.6 m). Leathery, shiny, handlike, deep green leaves, to 2 ft. (60 cm) wide, in flat rosettes of 7–15 leaflets, on woody leaf stalks. Flowers rare; grown for foliage. A related species, Hawaiian elf schefflera, *S. arboricola*, with smaller leaves, has similar care needs.

Conditions: Light: indirect sun, 6–8 hours daily. Humidity: 60–80%. Temperature: 55–70°F (13–21°C).

Soil: Well-drained, rich. 6.0–7.0 pH.

Care: Easy. Water to keep soil evenly moist; reduce watering in winter. Mist and wipe foliage occasionally. Fertilize at alternate waterings; dilute liquid fertilizer to half its recommended rate. Pinch growth tips to promote fullness. Prune to leaf axil 1 ft. (30 cm) above ground to renew. Repot semi-annually in spring. Propagate by stem cuttings, layering.

Features: Good choice for floors, landings in cool, tall-ceilinged rooms. Aphid, mealybug, scale, spider mite susceptible.

Name: Vase Plant; Queen's-Tears. *Billbergia* species. BROMELIACEAE.

Description: Many cultivars of slow-growing, radiating, tropical, epiphytic herbs, to 1 ft. (30 cm) tall and 3 ft. (90 cm) wide. Fleshy, shiny, straplike, deep green, pointed, finely toothed leaves, to 18 in. (45 cm) long, armed with spines. Pink edged with blue, green petaled flowers grow from pink, upright, arching bracts. Early summer blooming.

Conditions: Light: full or indirect sun, 8–10 hours daily. Humidity: 70–90%. Temperature: 60–80°F (16–27°C).

Soil: Well-drained, loose bark chips or slab with sphagnum moss. 5.5–6.5 pH.

Care: Easy. Apply demineralized water to central cup of plant. Mist sphagnum moss and foliage frequently. Fertilize semi-monthly with watering; dilute liquid fertilizer to a third of its recommended rate. Prune central plant foliage after flowering to develop new offsets. Repot annually, replacing bark. Propagate by offsets.

Features: Good choice for shallow bowls, tables, terrariums in contemporary, bright rooms. Mealybug, scale susceptible.

Name: Velvet Plant, Purple. *Gynura* species. ASTERACEAE (COMPOSITAE).

Description: Fast-growing, mounding or trailing, perennial, hairy, tropical herb, to 9 ft. (2.7 m) long outdoors, but indoors rarely over 4 ft. (1.2 m). Velvety, purple-haired, dagger-shaped, deep green, veined, scalloped leaves, to 8 in. (20 cm) long, with purple undersides. Multiple, yellow, dandelion-like flowers, with foul scent. Spring blooming. *G. aurantiaca* and *G. sarmentosa* are commonly cultivated.

Conditions: Light: filtered sun, 6–8 hours daily. Humidity: 60–80%. Temperature: 60–75°F (16–24°C) spring–autumn, 50–60°F (10–16°C) winter.

Soil: Well-drained, rich. 5.5–6.5 pH.

Care: Easy–moderate. Water to keep soil evenly moist during growth; reduce watering in winter. Avoid wetting foliage, misting. Fertilize with each watering; dilute acidic liquid fertilizer to half its recommended strength. Pick flowers at bud stage before scent develops. Pinch growth tips to promote fullness. Avoid pruning and repotting; propagate new plants. Propagate by stem cuttings.

Features: Good choice for hanging baskets, ledges, plant stands, windowsills in bright rooms, solariums. Good for color. Pest and disease resistant.

Name: Venus's-Flytrap. *Dionaea muscipula.* DROSERACEAE.

Description: Slow-growing, spreading, perennial, carnivorous herb, to 1 ft. (30 cm) tall. Shiny, green, oval, rounded leaves, to 3 in. (75 mm) long, in a flat rosette, plus specialized insect-trapping leaves on succulent stems bearing hairlike fringe and trigger cilia. When brushed, trap leaves quickly close. Multiple, white, flat flowers, to ¾ in. (19 mm) wide. Dormant in winter.

Conditions: Light: filtered sun to partial shade. Humidity: 70–90%. Temperature: 60–80°F (16–27°C).

Soil: Well-drained, sandy, average. 5.0–6.0 pH.

Care: Moderate–challenging. Water to keep soil very moist; use distilled or rain water. Avoid fertilizing. Feed with insects such as small moths; avoid feeding meat. Propagate by seeds.

Features: Good choice for terrariums in semi-shady, warm location. Good for children. Pest tolerant. Disease resistant.

Name: Wandering Jew; Purple Wandering Jew. *Tradescantia albiflora, T. fluminensis, T. zebrina.* COMMELINACEAE.

Description: Several closely related species with similar habits. Fast-growing, creeping or trailing, perennial, evergreen herbs, to 6 ft. (1.8 m) long. Velvety, tear-shaped, green, white, yellow, often variegated or striped, oval, pointed, leaves, to 3 in. (75 mm) long, some with purple, red veins and undersides. Multiple, white, sometimes pink, three-petaled flowers. Spring and autumn blooming.

Conditions: Light: filtered or indirect sun, 4–6 hours daily. Humidity: 40–60%. Temperature: 60–80°F (16–27°C) spring–autumn, 50–70°F (10–21°C) winter.

Soil: Well-drained, rich. 6.0–7.0 pH.

Care: Easy. Water when soil surface dries; reduce watering in winter. Fertilize with each watering; dilute liquid fertilizer to half its recommended rate. Pinch growth tips to direct growth. Prune severely to renew. Repot when roots become compacted in spring. Propagate by stem cuttings.

Features: Good choice for hanging baskets, plant stands, tables, windowsills in bathrooms, bright rooms, kitchens. Aphid, mealybug susceptible.

Name: Wax Plant; Honey Plant. *Hoya carnosa.* ASCLEPIADACEAE.

Description: Several cultivars of fast-growing, climbing, trailing, or twining, succulent, evergreen, vinelike shrub, to 20 ft. (6 m) tall or long. Shiny, waxy, fleshy, tear-shaped, green or variegated, pointed leaves, to 3 in. (75 mm) long, creased along their central vein. Globular clusters of waxy, fleshy, pink, white, fragrant flowers, to ⅝ in. (16 mm) wide, with red centers. Summer blooming.

Conditions: Light: filtered sun, 4–6 hours daily. Humidity: 40–70%. Temperature: 65–80°F (18–27°C) spring–autumn, 50–65°F (10–18°C) winter.

Soil: Well-drained, rich. 6.0–7.0 pH.

Care: Easy. Water when soil surface dries; reduce watering in winter. Fertilize with each watering. Stake on fibrous pole to support stems. Avoid deadheading spent flowers. Prune sparingly. Repot when roots become compacted in spring. Propagate by stem cuttings in spring.

Features: Good choice for hanging baskets, floors, ledges, windowsills in bathrooms, bright rooms. Mealybug, scale susceptible.

Name: Wood Sorrel; Lady's Sorrel; Irish Shamrock. *Oxalis acetosella.* OXALIDACEAE.

Description: Fast-growing, spreading, perennial, deciduous, rhizomatous bulb, to 6 in. (15 cm) tall. Velvety, cloverlike, deep or gray green leaves, to 3 in. (75 mm) wide, with red undersides, closing at night. Solitary, upturned, pink, white, yellow, funnel-shaped flowers, to 1 in. (25 mm) wide, with contrasting centers. Spring blooming.

Conditions: Light: partial shade. Humidity: 50–70%. Temperature: 40–75°F (4–24°C) during growth; store dormant rhizomes in dry soil in pot, 50–60°F (10–16°C).

Soil: Well-drained, rich–average. 6.5–7.5 pH.

Care: Easy. Water to keep soil evenly moist during growth. Withhold water for 4–6 weeks in late spring to force dormancy; store in pot, and repot annually in autumn. Fertilize at planting. Propagate by division, seed.

Features: Good choice for seasonal decoration, foliage in cool, low-light rooms. Leaves fold and close at night. Pest and disease resistant.

Name: Zebra Plant; Peacock Plant. *Calathea zebrina, C. makoyana.* MARANTACEAE.

Description: Slow-growing, branching or spreading, dense, perennial, tropical, evergreen herb, to 3 ft. (90 cm) tall. Satin-textured, deep green with olive-striped, oval, pointed leaves, to 2 ft. (60 cm) long and 1 ft. (30 cm) wide, with veins of yellow green and purple undersides. Flowers insignificant; grown for distinctive foliage. Closely related to *Ctenanthe, Maranta,* and *Stromanthe.*

Conditions: Light: indirect sun to partial shade. Humidity: 60–80%. Temperature: 65–75°F (18–24°C).

Soil: Well-drained, rich. 6.0–7.0 pH.

Care: Easy. Water to keep soil evenly moist; reduce watering in winter. Use dechlorinated or distilled water. Mass several plants in a stone-filled cachepot to add humidity. Fertilize with each watering spring–autumn; dilute liquid fertilizer to half its recommended strength. Protect from direct sun. Pinch growth points to direct growth. Repot when crowded in spring. Propagate by crown division, stem cuttings.

Features: Good choice for hanging baskets, columns, ledges in cool rooms, bathrooms. Good for color. Aphid, mealybug, spider mite susceptible.

ON-LINE INDEX

INDEX

INDEX